The Business Case for Corporate Social Responsibility

Philipp Schreck

The Business Case for Corporate Social Responsibility

Understanding and Measuring Economic Impacts of Corporate Social Performance

Physica-Verlag
A Springer Company

Dr. Philipp Schreck
Institute of Production Management
and Managerial Accounting
Ludwig-Maximilians-University Munich
Ludwigstr. 28
80539 Munich
Germany
schreck@bwl.lmu.de

ISBN 978-3-7908-2117-8 e-ISBN 978-3-7908-2118-5

DOI: 10.1007/978-3-7908-2118-5

Contributions to Management Science ISSN 1431-1941

Library of Congress Control Number: 2008940118

D19

Cover design: SPi Publisher Services

Printed on acid-free paper

9 8 7 6 5 4 3 2 1

springer.com

Foreword

Twenty years after the end of communism, problems of business ethics in capitalism have become increasingly important. Consequently, business ethics and Corporate Social Responsibility (CSR) have developed into highly debated and well-researched topics in Germany as well as internationally. Much of this work has been essentially normative. More recently, descriptive and empirical questions have gained increasing attention. In particular, researchers have sought empirical evidence for a business case for CSR, i.e. the notion that there is a positive relationship between corporate social and financial performance. Previous empirical investigations have failed to find a clear answer to that question. Mr. Schreck adds to this very exciting field of research by presenting and applying his own approach to such an empirical investigation. In particular, at least four elements of his approach are worth mentioning:

1. The author shows why previous investigations found contradictory results by assuming a direct relationship between corporate social performance and profit. In contrast to that, he develops a broader frame of reference which includes different and distinct components of CSR as well as several determinants of its relation to financial performance.
2. His empirical investigation's results are based on a new data base. Data are drawn from *oekom research* AG, which have not been used for scientifically rigorous studies till now. The work brings forward arguments to prove that these are more suitable than those of other comparable data banks.
3. Coupled to a conceptually sound study, the author uses a well developed econometric approach. This especially applies to his efforts to account for the widely neglected problem of endogeneity due to simultaneous causality between the social and financial performance of firms.
4. The empirical investigation produces several important results. Evidence is adduced that one cannot suppose a generic positive relation between CSR generally and profits. But there is evidence of such a relation for CSR's individual components. For example, consider corporate government and business ethics as well as environmental management. Another finding is that in contrast to what has often

been assumed from a neoclassical perspective, there is no significant negative relation between CSR and profit.

It is likely that the discussion on capitalism and ethics will continue. In my view, this must not only be done in terms of normative arguments, but should be grounded on empirical knowledge. Therefore the results of this study are an important base for practice and further research.

München
2008

Prof. Dr. Dr. h.c. Hans-Ulrich Küpper

Preface

Criticisms of the notion that companies should live up to and act in accordance with their social responsibilities, are probably as old as the idea itself. For a long time, economists in particular have fiercely argued against the concept of Corporate Social Responsibility (CSR) and warned that it would endanger the capitalist market system as a whole. Considering this hostile stance taken by some scholars in Germany as well as internationally, it is quite astonishing how business ethics in general and CSR in particular have managed to enter mainstream management research. Compared to international developments in business ethics, the German discussion has mainly occupied itself with normative questions such as whether and how companies could be expected to adhere to certain ethical standards, or whether business administration as an academic discipline should consider such questions at all. Conversely, descriptive research questions have not been that popular in the past and have only slowly started to form a legitimate part of business ethics and CSR research in Germany.

I have for a long time been very impressed by the sophisticated normative business ethics theories developed in continuation of the long-standing German tradition of ethical reasoning in philosophy, economics and business administration. Nonetheless, descriptive analysis is very important for normative theories, even and especially in the case of ethics (without necessarily being instrumental): normative theory in certain cases needs to know how things *actually work*, before it can determine how things *ought to work*. This doctoral thesis intends to contribute to an understanding of how CSR works. It does so by starting out with a very simple question (which, alas, does not stay that simple): Is there a business case for CSR? After writing this book, I wish I could say: CSR simply pays! As one might guess, it is not that easy. On the one hand, this is bad news because, if the story were that simple, there would be no reason to worry as companies, profit-seeking as they are, would just act in line with societal expectations. On the other hand, this is good news, as it leaves room for many more books and articles within this very exciting field of positive research.

This monograph was accepted as a doctoral thesis by the Munich School of Management at the Ludwig-Maximilians-University. It came into being during my work as a research and teaching assistant at the Institute of Operations Management and Managerial Accounting (IPC). I owe a great deal to many people at the institute who provided the perfect environment for me to start, advance and complete this project. First and foremost, I would like to express my deep gratitude to and respect for my doctoral supervisor Prof. Dr. Dr. h.c. Hans-Ulrich Küpper, who guided me through the sometimes very demanding process of overseeing a project such as this. He was always willing to discuss critically my thoughts at any stage of development, without curtailing too much my freedom to follow my personal preferences. His enthusiasm for ethical reasoning, his experience and his support, especially during the more critical periods, were of immense value to me. Beyond Prof. Küpper's professional supervision, he familiarised me with many academic and personal virtues, mostly through actions rather than words. This also applies to our research seminars (including some very fine skiing and hiking trips), which formed the ideal setting for the discussion of all our work in progress. Professionally and personally, I have benefited tremendously from my years at the IPC.

I am also indebted to the many colleagues that I have had the chance to work with at the IPC. I would first like to thank Prof. Dr. Gunther Friedl and Prof. Dr. Burkhard Pedell for their various comments and words of advice, which were of real help to me. My countless professional, and often personal and controversial, discussions with Dr. Kai Sandner helped me more than once to advance this thesis. Matthias Notz deserves many thanks for his ability to spread enthusiasm at the IPC and for countless helpful conversations. Special thanks also go to Wolfgang Götz for his unequalled Simpsons expertise, and for many legendary writing sessions in my kitchen. Finally, I owe my colleagues Claudia Gaier, Marion Rittmann, Christiane Romeo and Dr. Christian Lohmann thanks for the special atmosphere at the IPC; thanks also for the ladies' inexhaustible candy stocks.

I also wish to thank Prof. Dr. Ralf Elsas, the second referee of this thesis, who was always willing to provide me with very informed and helpful feedback and who repeatedly proved that it only takes a few minutes to ask questions that keep one busy for months. His comments and ideas contributed a great deal to this study. At Prof. Elsas' Institute of Finance and Banking, I owe thanks to Nadine Hadder and Christoph Breig as well, for helping me in my countless attempts to access their many useful databases. Furthermore, this thesis could not have been completed without the generous support of Matthias Bönning, head of research at *oekom research* AG. I owe him a debt of gratitude for allowing me the use of the company's core asset, its CSR ratings, and for being patient enough to answer even the most detailed (and sometimes hair-splitting) questions on the data's structure and nature.

My personal background has always formed the most important basis for my development, including that of my professional career; my family and friends therefore deserve my warmest thanks. This first applies to my parents and to my brother, Eric. It is impossible to express the gratitude that I feel towards my mother and father who have always loved and supported me in the pursuit of whatever idea came to my mind. I also wish to express my gratitude to my grandmother, Vera Schreck, for her continuous support and interest, and to my grandfather, Ludovic Farcas, who sadly passed away this year but had always been an example to me through his happiness, confidence and love of life. Very special thanks go to my best friends, of whom I can name only a few but who all helped me so much throughout the last few years, mostly without realising it. I owe a great deal to Jens for his intellectual input and our many shared experiences, as well as countless and invaluable advice and nargila-sessions; Max for Rock 'n' Roll and for being a truly exceptional friend; Miki for her unrivalled talent to unite chaos and clear thought; and Oliver for the longest and most continuous friendship I possess.

Last but not least I wish to express my deep gratitude to my girlfriend, Ursula, not only for her editorial contribution but most especially for her notoriously good humour, which formed an important counterpoint to many rather challenging moments, especially in the closing stages of this thesis. I will do my best to be of equal help to you in the coming months.

München
2008

Philipp Schreck

Contents

List of Abbreviations

CFP	Corporate Financial Performance
CRM	Customer Relationship Management
CRR	Corporate Responsibility Rating (*oekom research*)
CSP	Corporate Social Performance
CSR	Corporate Social Responsibility
EPS	Earnings per Share
ER	Environmental Rating (*oekom research*)
FE	Fixed Effects
FGLS	Feasible Generalised Least Squares
GLS	Generalised Least Squares
GMM	Generalised Method of Moments
IV	Instrumental Variable
KLD	Kinder, Lydenberg, Domini & Co.
NGO	Non-Governmental Organisation
OLS	Ordinary Least Squares
RE	Random Effects
ROA	Return on Assets
ROE	Return on Equity
ROI	Return on Investment
ROS	Return on Sales
SCR	Social Cultural Rating (*oekom research*)
SRI	Socially Responsible Investment
VIF	Variance Inflation Factor
2SLS	Two-Stage Least Squares

Chapter 1
The Economic Impact of Corporate Social Responsibility

1.1 Relevance of Measuring the Impact of CSR

Subsumed under the umbrella term Corporate Social Responsibility (CSR), the assumed duties of business in society have been an increasingly debated topic in academic research,[1] business practice,[2] politics[3] and media.[4] Especially within the scientific discussion, two contradicting positions can be distinguished: on the one hand, there is the argument that resources spent on other than economic goals are an illegitimate waste of resources, because they are contradictory to a firm's responsibility to its shareholders and therefore even to the very function of business in modern societies.[5] On the other hand, proponents of CSR try to champion their idea by emphasising the so-called *business case* for CSR. Arguing that CSR can come along with certain benefits that might outweigh its costs, they see CSR engagement as a necessity for business, not least for the sake of its own economic interest.[6]

---

[1] Cf. Crane et al. (2008); Crane and Matten (2004); Hansen and Schrader (2005); Kakabadse and Morsing (2006); Küpper (2006), p. 175; Schneider and Steiner (2004); Werther and Chandler (2006).

[2] See for instance German corporate initiatives such as *CSR Germany* (www.csrgermany.de) or *Econsense* (www.econsense.de), and *CSR Europe* (www.csreurope.org) or *Business for Social Responsibility* (www.bsr.org) on an international level.

[3] Cf. European Commission (2001); European Commission (2002); European Commission (2006); Riess (2006) for a recent overview.

[4] Throughout the last years, newspapers and magazines of all kinds have regularly published articles, surveys and special issues on CSR (e.g. *The Economist*, *The Financial Times* and *Handelsblatt*. For a comprehensive overview of CSR in the media, see www.csr-news.net). Moreover, the media has engaged in CSR rankings, cf. the *Manager Magazin*'s 'Good Company Ranking' and the issue from *Capital* (02/17/2005), including a similar ranking.

[5] Most prominently, Levitt (1958); Friedman (1962), p. 133; Friedman (1970); and – within the German context – Schneider (1990). For more recent arguments, see also Jensen (2002), p. 242; Henderson (2001); Sundaram and Inkpen (2004).

[6] Cf. Bowen (1953), p. 5; Brown and Fraser (2006); Drucker (1984); Freeman (1984); Hansen and Schrader (2005), pp. 383 et sqq.; Hoenicke (2002), p. 128; Kotler and Lee (2005), p. 21; Lohrie and Merck (2000), p. 44; Mintzberg (1983); Pierer (2002), p. 53; Porter and Kramer (2006);

P. Schreck, *The Business Case for Corporate Social Responsibility*, Contributions to Management Science.

This notion is of particular importance, because if CSR and profit maximising interests could indeed be shown to go hand in hand, two conflicts could be resolved. First, on a conceptual level, (economists') arguments against CSR as an illegitimate expenditure would lose their basis and two conflicting positions would eventually be united. Second, managers in practice could justify CSR expenses to the shareholders not only due to their moral quality but also with reference to their economic benefits. Similarly, investors would not have to worry about a trade-off between their hope for a maximum return on their investment on the one hand, and their ethical considerations on the other. However, as long as this parallelism of societal engagement and private business interests lacks empirical support, it risks corresponding to its advocates' wishful thinking rather than to a reliable fact that can serve as the ground for management decisions. Consequently, a profound understanding of CSR's economic impacts is highly relevant to both academic debate as well as practice.[7]

Given the importance of this question, it is not surprising that throughout the past decades a significant amount of research has been conducted on the empirical link between a firm's social and its financial performance (CFP/CSP-link).[8] In spite of its long-lasting tradition, however, this empirical research has not conclusively proven the aspiration that engagement in CSR *unconditionally* results in a win–win situation. In contrast, results of empirical studies have been very mixed so far.[9] As will be argued later, this ambiguity can be explained with reference to both the data employed in these studies and certain methodological differences that are so serious that they render the respective empirical results incomparable. Nevertheless, (meta-) studies have often treated previous results without taking these differences into account. Furthermore, this thesis will consider the search for a *universal* link between social and financial performance to be a misconception, which makes inconclusive results expectable rather than surprising. Taken together, this leaves room for further conceptual and empirical investigations into the conditions under which a positive link might exist.

1.2 Research Aim and Structure of the Thesis

The goal of this thesis is twofold. First, it aims at developing a thorough understanding of the mechanisms underlying the business case for CSR. This involves the analysis of why and under what circumstances investments into improved stakeholder relationships can be expected to come along with positive monetary

SustainAbility (edt., 2006), pp. 14 et sqq.; Utting (2005), pp. 378 et sqq.; World Business Council for Sustainable Development (2000).

[7] Considering the above said, talking about 'economic impacts' only refers to effects on the firm level, not all (macro-) economic effects possibly conceivable.

[8] Cf. Sect. 2.2.3.

[9] See for instance Utting (2000), p. 20; or the discussion about a positive correlation between corporations' corporate social and its financial performance in Margolis and Walsh (2003).

net benefits.[10] Taking into account relevant theoretical work on CSR and earlier empirical studies, such an analysis is indispensable to justify the assumption of a CSP/CFP-link before testing it empirically. Second, the thesis will use the results of the preceding analysis for an empirical investigation into the relationship that a given firm's CSR performance has with its economic performance. Besides methodological differences to already existing works, the study will employ new and arguably more reliable data derived from the CSR ratings of the German rating agency *oekom research*.

An empirical analysis of CSR practices differs from a normative analysis, in that it descriptively asks what kind of responsibility companies *actually do* take, and what consequences this engagement has from the firm's perspective. This thesis will not consider the normative question whether or not corporations *ought to* be assumed to have social responsibilities, though very important from a societal point of view. That is, the following analysis does not focus on *reasons for*, but on *impacts of* firm responses to certain admitted responsibilities; its aim is therefore mainly descriptive.[11]

Corresponding to the research aim just outlined, the analysis proceeds in two main steps. Chapter 2 intends to develop a frame of reference for the subsequent empirical investigation. It does so by reviewing conceptual works first on responsibility in general and then on CSR in particular. Based on this analysis, it will critically examine existing empirical work on the CSP/CFP-link and explain why it is not surprising that this research stream has so far failed to yield consistent results. The discussion will then lead to conclusions concerning the further procedure in Chap. 3.

The empirical analysis in that part begins by asking which determinants have an influence on whether companies perform high on the oekom corporate responsibility rating. Besides analysing these drivers of the companies' over-all social performance, it also scrutinises whether results change after breaking down the analysis into a social and an environmental component of CSR. The major part of the investigation will then focus on possible relations between corporate social and financial performance. After a cross-sectional analysis of this relation, it will specify some econometric problems associated with such analyses and examine the severity of these problems within the dataset. Finally, a dynamic perspective is brought into the analysis by examining whether results change when data from two different points in time are considered. Chapter 4 will draw final conclusions and give an outlook on the need for further research and implications for managers and investors.

---

[10] Section 2.1.3 includes the discussion of the relation between CSR and the stakeholder approach.

[11] However, this work necessarily includes normative elements: evaluating how well companies manage to deal with their responsibilities includes judgements, which is in itself normative due to the underlying values, upon which the judgement is based, see Küpper (2006), pp. 43–47.

Chapter 2
A Framework for Analysing Economic Impacts of Corporate Social Performance

Before examining the economic impacts of superior corporate social performance, this chapter intends to provide an analysis of both conceptual work on CSR and previous empirical studies that have addressed similar questions in the past. To develop such a frame of reference, it should first be explicated what exactly is meant by the concept of CSR. Therefore, Sect. 2.1 deals with past efforts to define CSR, and with their limitations for the specific purposes of this thesis. Section 2.2 reviews empirical studies on the relationship between corporations' social and financial performance and tries to explain why it so far has failed to come to clear results as to the existence, strength and direction of such a link. Subsequently, Sect. 2.3 draws conclusions from this review and proposes some results concerning a methodology for an empirical analysis of the economic firm-level effects of corporate social performance.

2.1 Concepts of Corporate Social Issues: From CSR to CSP

Though widely used in theory and practice, the term corporate social responsibility (CSR) has been notoriously difficult to define ever since. The broadness of the term, though sometimes at its advantage, has also been seen as its major drawback, as Votaw's often-cited criticism illustrates:

> "The term is a brilliant one; it means something, but not always the same thing, to everybody. To some it conveys the idea of legal responsibility or liability; to others it means socially responsible behavior in an ethical sense; to still others, the meaning transmitted is that of 'responsible for', in a causal mode; many simply equate it with a charitable contribution."[1]

A proper understanding of CSR is of a certain importance, as it allows for the judgement whether or not a given corporate action can be classified as part of its

---

[1] Votaw (1973) p. 11. For a harsh critique of the concept's "analytical looseness and lack of rigor", see Friedman (1970), p. 156.

P. Schreck, *The Business Case for Corporate Social Responsibility*,
Contributions to Management Science.

social performance, which becomes especially relevant when intending to measure its economic impact.

2.1.1 Responsibility as a Multi-Relational Concept

In order to come to a clear understanding of what is meant by CSR, the philosophical discussion on the concept of responsibility can deliver first valuable insights. In philosophy, the exact meaning of the term responsibility has for long been a popular topic of debate.[2] In spite of many controversies, there seems to be agreement concerning two aspects that are of special relevance for the investigation of CSR.

First, slight differences in the exact wording notwithstanding, philosophers agree that the term responsibility can be used with different connotations. It can either merely describe a causal relationship,[3] e.g. when cold temperatures are responsible for slippery streets. It can further mean a positive judgement of a person's praiseworthy character, which is for instance the case when saying that "this women is a responsible person."[4] Finally, it can be used in the sense of personal responsibility.[5] In that understanding, a person (or institution) is held accountable for his or her behaviour or a certain state of affairs. Within the last category, responsibility can be further differentiated into two sub-categories.[6] On the one hand, prospective responsibility concerns a person's responsibilities lying in the future, e.g. when the lifeguard is responsible for the swimmers' lives. Retrospective responsibility, on the other hand, means a person's accountability for actions and/or its consequences. If, for example, a swimmer drowns in presence of a lifeguard, the latter is held responsible for not having saved the swimmer's life.

A second common ground within the philosophical literature on responsibility lies in the fact that it is a multi-relational concept with at least three elements. According to the minimum definition, it contains a subject/carrier (who is responsible?), an object (what for?) and an authority (to whom?) of responsibility.[7] Other definitions include a fourth element by further asking for the normative criteria on grounds of which responsibility is ascribed.[8] Applied to the CSR context, such a

---

[2] For an overview concerning the contentious issues, see Lenk and Maring (2004); Oshana (1997); Strawson (1994); Watson (1996); Werner (2002), pp. 524 et sqq.; Zimmerman (2001), pp. 1487 et sqq.

[3] Werner (2002), p. 522; Zimmerman (2001), p. 1486.

[4] See Oshana (1997), p. 71; Werner (2002), p. 522.

[5] See Oshana (1997), p. 71; Werner (2002), pp. 521 et seq.; Zimmerman (2001), p. 1486.

[6] See Werner (2002), pp. 521 et seq.; Zimmerman (2001), p. 1486. One could also perceive of retrospective and prospective versions of a causal and a judgement understanding of responsibility. This differentiation, however, does not appear in the cited literature.

[7] See Zimmerli (1992), p. 102.

[8] For definitions that are based on four and more elements see Höffe (1993), p. 23; Küpper (2006), pp. 181 et sqq.; Lenk and Maring (2004), p. 1558; Ropohl (1994), p. 111 et seq.; Werner (2002), p. 522.

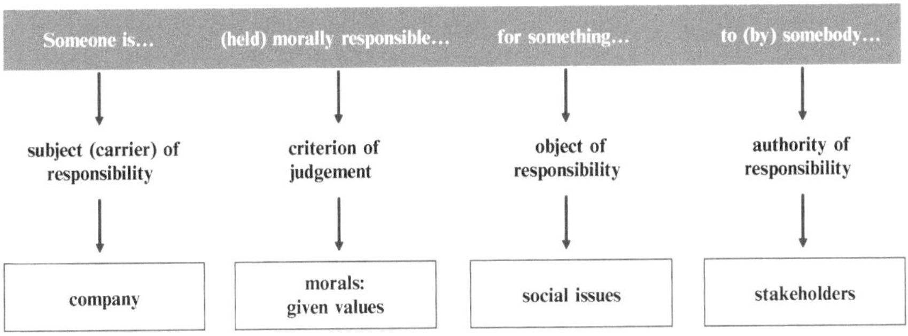

Fig. 2.1 Corporate social responsibility as a multi-relational concept

definition, as shown in Fig. 2.1, translates to the following statement: A *company* (subject/carrier) is held *morally* (normative standard) responsible *for something* (object) *by somebody* (authority).

For the time being, this concept is merely a formal but "empty" scheme as regards content.[9] However, this scheme can serve as a frame of reference for the further analysis of CSR. The first element, the subject of responsibility, does not need specific elaboration here, as it clearly refers to the company.[10] The same applies to the normative standard. Law, social roles, and morals are three important criteria of responsibility.[11] In the case of social responsibility, people judge companies on the ground of morals, understood as the totality of norms and values holding for a given society.[12] Due to the descriptive research aim of this paper, the normative discussion of prevailing norms and values itself is not part of further analysis. Relevant to this study is the fact that companies *are* judged on the ground of morals, regardless of the concrete nature of these norms and values. The remainder of this chapter therefore focuses on the object and the authority of responsibility, before it finally summarises the main insights for further analysis.

2.1.2 The Object of Responsibility: What are Companies Held Responsible for?

2.1.2.1 Responsibility as a Matter of Ascription

Given the assumption that corporations can generally be held responsible, it still has to be answered *for which issues* that happens. In normative discussions about

[9] Cf. Lenk and Maring (2004), p. 1558.

[10] Concerning the debate whether corporations can be held responsible as collective actors see Donahue (1991); Goodpaster and Matthews (1982); Küpper (2006), p. 185.

[11] Cf. Küpper (2006), p. 186.

[12] Cf. Küpper (2006), p. 13.

responsibility, a causal relation between the subject's action and the object of responsibility is often seen as a necessary condition for the ascription of responsibility:

> "Furthermore, for an unambiguous and unequivocal ascription of responsibility it seems to be necessary that the matter in question *has been caused* by the decision or action."[13]

Though this might hold true in the case of normative discussions on responsibility ("who can legitimately be held responsible?"), descriptive concepts of CSR that demand such a causal relationship fall short of embracing the entirety of observable phenomena with regards to CSR. As can be seen from both the different facets of the philosophical concept of responsibility as well as from the definition of the term as a multi-relational concept, responsibility is an inherent matter of ascription, i.e. persons and institutions do not necessarily bear responsibility *per se*, but they are *held responsible*.[14] As a matter of fact, society *de facto* places social responsibilities on companies even in cases where they undoubtedly did not cause the problems in question (which, of course, does not mean that they could not contribute to the amelioration of these problems). Such ascriptions of responsibilities then do not refer to the company's role in the emergence of problems (causal relation), but in their ability to solve already existing problems. Companies, their "causal innocence" notwithstanding, *do* agree in some cases to contribute to the amelioration of these problems and in that way *do* live up to the ascribed responsibilities. This shows that causal responsibility for a given problem is neither a necessary nor a sufficient condition for the actual ascription of responsibilities. The classification depicted in Fig. 2.2 illustrates the independence of a causal relation and *de facto* ascription of responsibilities.

Regardless of their causal responsibility, in each of the situations located in quadrants *I*, *II*, and *IV*, the company faces the question of how to respond to its (ascribed) responsibilities. However, an empirical analysis of economic consequences of a good performance with regards to CSR only has to take into account cases *I* and *IV*, because *III* does not involve any kind of responsibility, and quadrant *II* refers to situations, where companies are not held responsible for certain issues, although being causally responsible for them. This is for instance the case when social issues, such as the violation of human rights in production facilities or environmental pollution, are not detected by the public. In the context of personal responsibility, this quadrant includes examples where somebody presumably did not deliberately choose the action he had taken; i.e. if he was forced to take the action in question or if he was not in his right mind. Field *I* represents a fit between causality and the ascription of responsibility, which is for instance the case when companies in heavy-polluting industries agree to adhere to environmental standards exceeding those required by

---

[13] Küpper (2006), p. 190 (italics added, my translation). See also Göbel (2006), p. 101 for the necessity of a causal relation, and Fitch (1976), p. 38, who bases his definition of CSR on such a causal relation.

[14] See also Küpper (2006), pp. 181 and 185; Lenk and Maring (2004), p. 1558; Oshana (1997); Werner (2002), p. 521; Wieland (1999), p. 16; Zimmerman (2001), p. 1486 et seq.

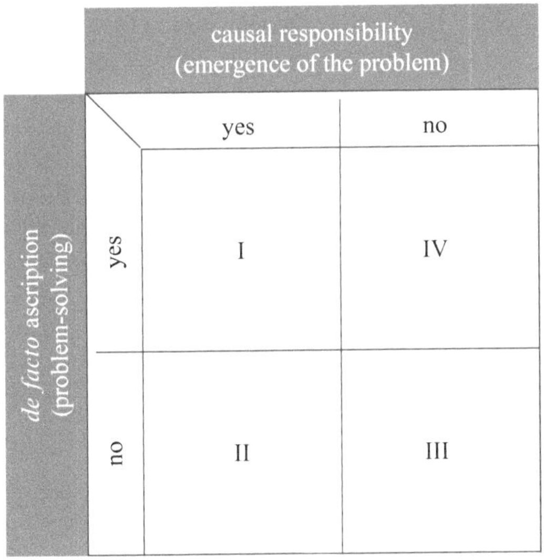

Fig. 2.2 Responsibilities possibly ascribed to companies

law. Quadrant *IV* refers to the aforementioned cases where companies are pushed to help change certain conditions in spite of the absence of a causal relation between the subject (the company) and the object (conditions). Examples for such demands include the corporations' efforts to fight against Apartheid in South Africa until the early 1990s,[15] their contribution to the achievement of the UN Millennium Development Goals, or engagement for an ethical development of regulatory frameworks.[16] The reason for the rise of such demands mainly can be seen in the failure of those public institutions that were hitherto in charge of such problems. As (especially multinational) companies are then perceived to be the most powerful private actors, they are seen as a promising way to fight diseases, run educational programs or even grant civil rights and stabilise democratic institutions.[17] It can therefore be assumed that it is the company's ability to solve problems rather than its causal responsibility for them that sometimes leads to the ascription of responsibilities.[18] All of these corporate activities then represent reactions to (ascribed) social responsibilities which are perceived by stakeholders inside and outside the organisation. Therefore, they should have an impact on the company's financial performance, which in turn can be analysed empirically.

---

[15] KLD, a CSR rating agency, even used "South African Involvement" as one criterion for the assessment of a company's social performance, see Sharfman (1996), pp. 288 et sqq.

[16] See Scherer et al. (2006); Hansen and Schrader (2005), p. 376.

[17] See Davis (1960); Matten and Crane (2005), pp. 169 et sqq.

[18] See Friedman (1970), p. 158 and Küpper (2006), pp. 184 and 189.

2.1.2.2 What is *Social* About CSR? On the Search for the Defining Criterion

If it is clear that so-called social responsibilities are ascribed to business, the question remains what it exactly is that makes a responsibility a social one. At the core of most, if not all, definitions of CSR lies the idea that actions and decisions by a company do not only concern its own interests but also those of society as a whole, or in economic terms: companies should internalise negative external effects. Howard Bowen, who is – in spite of early writings on corporations' social responsibilities in the 1920s[19] – widely recognised as the first influential scholar addressing CSR, states that it

> "...refers to the obligations of businessmen to pursue those policies, to make those decisions, or to follow those lines of action which are desirable in terms of the objectives and values of our society."[20]

Those societal "objectives and values" can mean, for instance, that companies are expected to ensure certain environmental standards reaching beyond those defined by law, to ensure occupational health and safety standards in the absence of formal regulation (especially in outsourced production sites in developing countries), to engage in the local community (by sponsoring charity projects or investing in education)[21] and to avoid unethical business practices such as bribing.

Still, the reference to societal values leaves the question unanswered what precisely constitutes the very nature of corporations' *social* responsibilities and their efforts to live up to it. How can a certain corporate action or decision be attributed to the company's social responsibility? No consent has been reached as to this question, and in the light of failed efforts to define CSR, some even conclude that it "...has become difficult, if not impossible, to define what is, or what is not, a social issue."[22] Many answers to this question exist in efforts to define the concept of CSR, which – in spite of many intersections – can conceptually be differentiated by looking at the criterion upon which they base their definition.

Some definitions require that CSR reaches beyond the legal and economic obligations of a company and therefore imply that voluntarism is a characteristic feature of CSR.[23] Focusing on legal aspects, this means that

---

[19] See Carroll (1999), p. 269; Windsor (2001), p. 229; Wood and Jones (1995), p. 233.

[20] Bowen (1953), p. 6. For other definitions of CSR that focus on the public interest, see Davis (1973), pp. 312 et seq.; Eells and Walton (1974), p. 247; Frederick (1960), p. 60; Frederick (1994), p. 150; Hansen and Schrader (2005), pp. 376 et seq.; Jones (1980), pp. 59 et seq.; Lerner and Fryxell (1988), p. 952; McGuire (1963), p. 144; McWilliams and Siegel (2001), p. 117; Steinmann (1973), pp. 467 et seq.; Zenisek (1979), p. 366.

[21] The latter examples are often called "social" responsibilities, i.e. concerning human society as opposed to the natural environmental. Compared to the comprehensive meaning of CSR, this represents a restricted understanding of the word "social". In order to avoid confusion between those two understandings, this paper uses the word in the comprehensive sense only.

[22] Clarkson (1995), p. 102.

[23] For such definitions see Davis and Blomstrom (1966), p. 12; Eells and Walton (1974), p. 247; European Commission (2006), p. 2; Jones (1980), p. 60; McGuire (1963), p. 144; McWilliams and Siegel (2001), p. 117; Sethi (1975), pp. 62 and 70; Walton (1967), p. 18.

"... social responsibility begins where the law ends. A firm is not being socially responsible if it merely complies with the minimum requirements of the law, because this is what any good citizen would do."[24]

Although beyond compliance firm behaviour might be a good indicator for socially responsible behaviour, it is critical to assume that CSR starts only where the law ends. Breaching the law is often a topic of CSR debates, as the examples of reporting scandals[25] or corruption[26] show. Hence, the law hardly allows for a sharp distinction between social and other responsibilities. With regards to economic aspects, the problem with voluntarism is that it is difficult to assess whether decisions in organisations indeed include the consideration of obligations beyond economic interests. To answer this question, CSR definitions have pointed at either decision-makers' motives or the effects of corporate action.

As one possibility to judge why actions are taken, early scholars tried to define CSR by asking for the "real" motives and intentions underlying decisions in business. The decision-maker's consideration of public interests is then seen as a necessary and sufficient condition for classifying a *social* decision. Actions labelled "social" but taken as a means to economic ends, then cannot belong to CSR, as in "its purest form, social responsibility is supported for its own sake because that is the noble way for corporations to behave."[27] One definition focusing directly on the managers' interests comes from Johnson (1971) who states that a "socially responsible entrepreneur or manager is (...) *interested* not only in his own well-being but also in that of the other members of the enterprise and that of his fellow citizens."[28] And Davis and Blomstrom (1971) see the "true test of social responsibility [in] whether issues of public interest are *considered at the time a decision is made*. If so, social responsibility is involved."[29] A closer analysis, however, shows that motives can hardly serve as an adequate defining criterion for CSR, as intentions are not directly observable and are therefore extremely difficult to assess.[30] Furthermore, corporate decisions "may have multiple rather than single motives and, therefore, this is not a fruitful criterion for judging social responsibility."[31] One could instead rely upon corporate communication as a proxy for the actual intentions, but it may

---

24 Davis (1973), p. 312. For other definitions of CSR as going beyond legal requirements, see Jones (1980), pp. 59 et seq.; McWilliams and Siegel (2001), p. 117; Vogel (2005), p. 2.

25 Cf. Tonge et al. (2003) on the Enron Case.

26 Cf. Rodriguez et al. (2006). For articles taking legal compliance as a proxy for socially responsible behaviour, see Wood and Jones (1995), p. 255.

27 Mintzberg (1983), p. 3.

28 Johnson (1971), p. 68 (italics added).

29 Davis and Blomstrom (1971), p. 87 (italics added). For other definitions based on motives and interests, see Backman (1975), p. 2; Davis (1960), p. 70; Davis (1973), p. 312 et seq.; Walton (1967), p. 18.

30 Concerning the difficulties to find out the "real" motives of CSR, see also Carroll (1999), p. 276 and Manne and Wallich (1972), p. 8.

31 Carroll (1999), p. 276. For similar criticism see Bowman (1973), p. 42; Picot (1977), p. 24; Windsor (2001), p. 226.

be doubted that this is a reliable procedure. Firm representatives will always tend to emphasize the societal benefits of corporate social programs rather than their economically benign effects for the company itself. Some go even so far as to say that such claims hint at exactly the opposite motives: "[M]anagers must *say* that they are responsible, because they are *not*."[32]

Instead of asking for motives and interests being considered at the time a decision is taken, one can also analyse the effects[33] of certain corporate actions in order to evaluate whether they reach beyond economic obligations. The problem with defining CSR this way is that it neglects multiple effects of an action. If, for instance, high environmental standards lead to a good reputation which in turn raises the brand value, it is hard to assess due to which effect the high standards were installed. Certain authors therefore even require that "true" CSR comes along with economic losses:

> "To qualify as socially responsible corporate action, a business expenditure or activity must be one for which the *marginal returns to the corporation are less than the returns available from some alternative expenditure*, must be purely voluntary, and must be an actual corporate expenditure rather than a conduit for individual largesse."[34]

However, financial harm as the defining criterion bears some problems for both conceptual as well as empirical reasons. In economics, the independence of motives (private gain) and outcomes (public wealth) has a long tradition. Adam Smith emphasised that the praiseworthy effects of competitive markets can be expected *independently of whether the economic agents have them in mind*.[35] It is the prospects of private gain that drives their economic behaviour rather than their consideration of social needs. In this context, Karl Homann and Ingo Pies point at the beneficial, though not-intended consequences of self-centred actions.[36] Definitions of CSR that rely on material losses ignore and even exclude this convergence of private and public gain. Furthermore, especially relevant to the aim of this paper, empirical criticism can be brought forward against such definitions. In case of the measurement of economic impacts of CSR practices, demanding for financial harm would imply the expectation of a negative link between CSR and financial measures *ex definitione*. Such a definition would therefore render empirical tests of the business case hypothesis impossible, as the latter assumes that CSR efforts can have positive impacts on financial measures.

As the analysis above has shown, neither legal/economic voluntarism nor motives nor effects serve as adequate criteria, as long as they are dependent on the identification of the 'real' motives or the 'either economic or social' outcomes. CSR

---

[32] Cheit (1964), p. 172 (italics in original).

[33] See, e.g. Davis and Blomstrom (1966), p. 12.

[34] Manne and Wallich (1972), p. 4–6 (italics added). For another definition focusing on the costs of CSR see Browne and Haas (1974), p. 48.

[35] Cf. the famous passage from Smith (1991), p. 20, in which the role of economic agents' self interest in markets is discussed.

[36] Cf. Homann and Pies (1994), p. 8.

definitions that rely on such criteria of distinction are deemed to fail because they ignore multiple motives and effects of corporate actions: "Economic" actions can have ethically benign outcomes, and "ethically motivated" decisions can have financially sound effects. A clear separation of social from economically rational decisions is therefore not possible.[37]

2.1.2.3 Analytical Frameworks as Definitions of CSR

Partly as a response to the inherent difficulties of the concept of CSR, efforts shifted to defining CSR by offering frameworks that help analyse CSR practices. Along with this development the point of interest moved to the scrutiny of how companies react to these ascribed responsibilities and thereby focused on processes and outcomes. This reaction was then labelled *Corporate Social Performance* (CSP).

Carroll (1979) first presented his CSP model that includes the three dimensions *Social Responsibility Categories* (which were meant to define CSR), *Social Issues Involved* (an enumeration of issues such as the natural environment or product safety), and *Philosophy of Social Responsiveness* (asking how the company reacts to ascribed responsibilities).[38] Interestingly, by encompassing the "economic, legal, ethical, and discretionary[39] expectations that society has of organizations at a given point in time",[40] this approach tries to separate economic from legal and ethical responsibilities and therefore cannot avoid any of the definitional problems discussed above. Furthermore, it comes along with an additional problem when it ought to be measured against indicators of financial performance. If CSR comprises economic responsibilities per definition, then a comparison between a company's social and its financial performance at least partly would mean measuring variables against themselves.[41]

Nevertheless, Carroll's model served as the blueprint for several subsequent definitions and analytical frameworks of CSP. At the base of each of these concepts lies the distinction between three different dimensions, mainly oriented at Carroll's model (see Fig. 2.3). Wartick and Cochran (1985) with their widely cited definition talk of *principles*, *policies* and *processes*. Wood (1991a), sees CSP as

---

[37] For definitions of CSR stating that turning social problems into private profits *is* the corporation's *social* responsibility, see Drucker (1984), p. 62; Friedman (1970); Friedman (1962), p.133; Johnson (1971), p. 54.

[38] See Carroll (1979), p. 503.

[39] The fourth category was later called "philanthropic", see Carroll (1991b), p. 42, and finally merged with the ethical category into a three domains-approach, see Schwartz and Carroll (2003). These changes, however, did not reflect any substantial conceptual differences.

[40] Carroll (1979), p. 500 (footnote added).

[41] Consequently, in the first attempt to apply Carroll's CSP model for the measurement of the link between CSR and firm profitability, Aupperle et al. (1985) excluded the economic dimension from their operationalisation of CSR, which is a contradiction to their own definition.

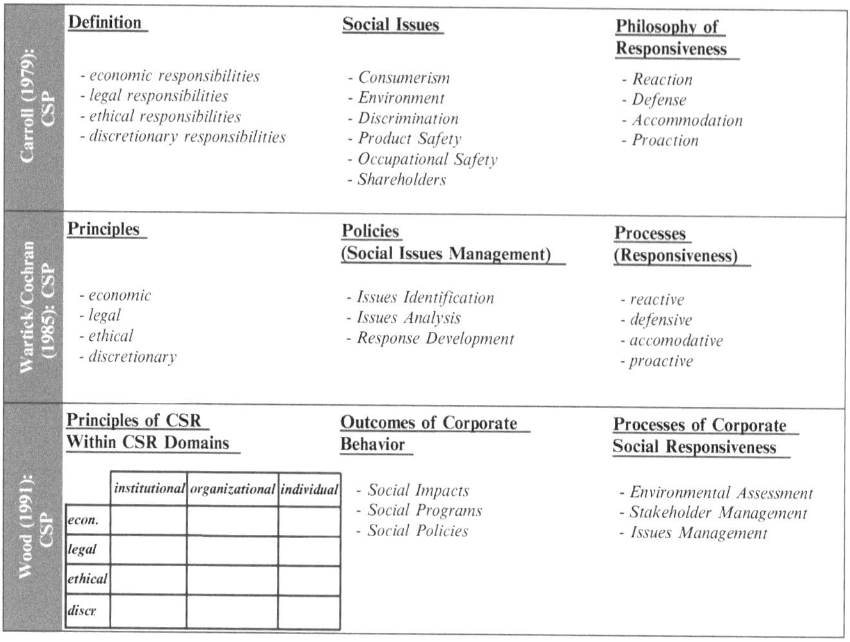

Fig. 2.3 Definitions of corporate social performance (CSP)

"... a business organization's configuration of *principles* of social responsibility, *processes* of social responsiveness, and policies, programs, and observable *outcomes* as they relate to the firm's societal relationships."[42]

These frameworks allow for a more facetted understanding of CSP, which is able to organise various related aspects for instance by looking at which stakeholder is involved, how the company reacts (policies & processes), or at which level (individual, organisational, institutional) this takes place. But the question what a "social" issue is, still remains. Therefore, the CSP frameworks might provide valuable insights for the conceptual analysis of corporate social action, and reorient further analysis by framing and integrating[43] existing research in the field of business and society. But their first dimension – be it called "definition" or "principles" – still implicitly needs a judgement of what a social issue is. As the concepts in this context all draw on Carroll's four categories, the criticism brought forward above equally applies to the later models of CSP. In this respect, they offer little guidance as to the quantitative measurement of CSP.

[42] Wood (1991a), p. 693 (italics added); see also Swanson (1995), p. 43, who uses exactly the same terminology. For a slightly different approach see Epstein (1987), p. 104, who sees business ethics, corporate social responsibility and corporate social responsiveness as three elements of a "corporate social policy process".

[43] For a framework attempting to integrate descriptive and normative work on CSP, see Swanson (1999).

2.1.3 *The Authority of Responsibility: By whom are Corporations Held Responsible?*

Closely related to asking *for what* corporations are responsible, is the question concerning the authority of responsibility: *To whom* are corporations responsible? Put differently and applied to the descriptive aim of this paper: *By whom* are responsibilities ascribed to corporations? The Stakeholder Approach, first so labelled by Edward R. Freeman,[44] is still a widely discussed concept which offers a helpful heuristic to categorise, sort and analyse multiple interests concerned by an organisation.[45] As mentioned above, it was therefore used in the Wood (1991a) model to specify "processes of corporate social responsiveness" which include, amongst others, stakeholder management.[46]

By definition, a stakeholder is "any group or individual who can affect or is affected by the achievement of the organization's objectives."[47] This definition shows that companies face various different stakeholders' interests that are occasionally at conflict with each other or with the company's (i.e. the shareholders') own interests. Therefore, one can describe CSR as the challenge of "managing a multiplicity of interests."[48] When companies are asked to, or they themselves claim to act in a socially responsible way, this always hints at the existence of conflicting interests of different stakeholders. By clarifying whose interests are possibly at conflict, the stakeholder concept helps to put the concept of CSR into concrete terms.

Examples of stakeholders include employees, customers, shareholders, suppliers & subcontractors, the community in which the company operates, governments and non-governmental organisations (NGOs), often representing other stakeholders' interests that cannot be brought forward by themselves. This is for instance the case with the natural environment, animals or future generations. As these examples make clear, the stakeholders that are affected by the company and those that ascribe responsibilities to it, do not necessarily have to be identical.

Within the literature on the stakeholder approach, three different and distinct strands can be identified:[49]

- *Normative* concepts: To which stakeholders' interests *should* companies pay attention?
- *Descriptive* concepts: To which stakeholders' interests and in which way *do* managers pay attention?

---

[44] Cf. Freeman (1984).

[45] For recent discussions and developments, see Donaldson and Preston (1995); Freeman (1999); Freeman (2004); Jensen (2002); Jones et al. (2002); Mitchell et al. (1997); Phillips et al. (2003); Ulrich (1999).

[46] For an adoption of the Wood-model from a stakeholder theory perspective see Clarkson (1991) and Clarkson (1995).

[47] Freeman (1984), p. 46.

[48] Johnson (1971), p. 51.

[49] See Donaldson and Preston (1995), pp. 66 et seq.

- *Instrumental* concepts: *What happens*, if companies pay attention to certain stakeholders' interests in certain ways?

For the purpose of this paper, descriptive and instrumental aspects of the stakeholder concept are most relevant. As mentioned before, in contrast to a philosophical normative analysis, the question here is not which responsibilities companies *should* theoretically bear, but which ones are *de facto* ascribed to corporations and what impact their consideration has. Therefore, the normative question of whether or not stakeholder claims are deemed legitimate in an objective sense is not the point of interest here.[50] That makes it understandable why (instrumental) stakeholder approaches are so widely used in empirical research on CSP.[51]

2.1.4 Results for Further Analysis

As the analysis above has shown, efforts to define CSR come along with certain insurmountable difficulties. None of the commonly used criteria – neither the scope of law, motives underlying corporate decisions, nor the effects of their actions – can serve as an unequivocal basis for a precise definition of CSR. The subsequently developed CSP models offer useful frames of reference, but are not able to overcome the definitional problems of earlier concepts. In the light of these sobering results, conceptual attempts should be formulated moderately. Instead of asking for a universal definition of CSR, a workable concept should be proposed according to the respective research aim. Applied to the investigation of the CSP/CFP link, such a concept would have to include the following insights:

1. As visualised in Fig. 2.1, CSR is a multi-relational concept, which – if empirical effects of CSP are at interest – is therefore inherently a matter of ascription.
2. Such ascriptions of social responsibilities take place on the basis of moral standards as normative criteria of judgement. Based on such criteria, stakeholders internal and external to the organisation perceive value conflicts and sometimes hold the company responsible for their solution, independently of whether or not a causal relation exists between the company and the problem at hand.
3. The analysis of the literature has revealed no unanimous and unambiguous answer considering the exact scope of CSR. With regards to the purpose of this paper, it is therefore advisable to address the question of whether or not a given corporate action builds part of CSR empirically rather than conceptually. An understanding of CSR can be gained by looking at what kind of value conflicts lead to moral claims being directed at companies, and at their reactions.

---

[50] Concerning aspects of stakeholder legitimacy, see Donaldson and Preston (1995), pp. 73 et sqq.; Mitchell et al. (1997), pp. 872 et sqq.; Ulrich (1999), pp. 37–44.

[51] For empirical studies using stakeholder theory as a frame of reference, see Mitchell et al. (1997); Rowley (1997); Berman et al. (1999); Hillman and Keim (2001); Graves and Waddock (2000); Harrisson and Freeman (1999); Ogden and Watson (1999); Ruf et al. (2001); Wood and Jones (1995).

4. Even though it is hardly possible to define its exact scope, CSR is a multidimensional concept due to its involvement of various stakeholders' interests.
5. Descriptive and instrumental aspects of the Stakeholder Approach help sorting the issues at question as it allows for an analysis of who ascribes social responsibilities, and who is affected if the company reacts.[52]
6. Consequently, so-called social issues can vary over time due to changes in culture, problems, and legal regulation. Hence, empirical analyses are *status quo* descriptions, which implies temporal limits to their validity.

Based on the conceptual literature on CSR and in an attempt to identify what is meant by corporate social performance, the analysis to this point has proposed a number of preliminary results. As the research aim of this thesis is the inquiry of the empirical relation between corporations' social and their financial performance, the following chapter reviews already existing studies on this relationship and forms the basis for a critical examination in Sect. 2.3.

2.2 Measuring Economic Impacts: Empirical Studies on the CSP/CFP-Link

2.2.1 Corporate Social Performance: Remarks on Related Terms

Not all of the studies described in the following use the same wording, though they refer to similar underlying concepts. Therefore, some clearing remarks as to various concepts frequently brought forward in the *Business and Society* literature are appropriate at this point in order to avoid confusion. *Corporate Social Responsibility* (CSR) concerns the question discussed above, what kinds of social responsibilities can be and actually are ascribed to corporations. This term then falls into the earlier described category of personal responsibility.[53] The *Stakeholder Approach*, as mentioned, clarifies the concept of CSR by categorising and sorting the allocations of social responsibilities.[54] *Corporate Social Performance* (CSP), as does *Corporate Social Responsiveness*,[55] refers to the company's response to the assigned responsibilities. It concerns the extent to which – judged from an external point of view – the firm meets the expectations related to these responsibilities. Understood this way, the term corresponds to the understanding of the term "responsible" as a

[52] From this perspective, improved CSP can either mean that the accepted responsibilities are extended by new constituencies (i.e. hitherto not considered stakeholders such as the natural environment, animals, or the community) or that the responsibility towards certain stakeholders is widened by certain aspects (e.g. in the case of employees: job security, co-determination, etc.).

[53] Cf. Fig. 2.1 on p. 7.

[54] See Velamuri and Freeman (2006) for an effort to merge CSR and Stakeholder Theory into the concept of "Corporate Stakeholder Responsibility".

[55] Cf. Ackerman and Bauer (1976); Frederick (1994), p. 154 et sqq.; Frederick (1998); Lerner and Fryxell (1988), p. 952.

judgement of a character.[56] A number of other concepts, though frequently used in academia as well as in practice, do not offer any explanations that go substantially beyond those of the above mentioned concepts. The notion that companies ought to subscribe to the ideas *Sustainable Development*,[57] *Corporate Citizenship*,[58] *Social Issues Management*[59] or a *Triple Bottom Line*[60] basically all refer to the extension of corporate responsibilities by societal values and therefore only include issues already subsumed to the concept of CSR.

2.2.2 The Empirical Investigation of the CSP/CFP-Link as an Important Topic in Management Research

For more than 30 years, the existence, direction, and strength of a possible link between corporate social performance (CSP) and corporate financial performance (CFP) have been subject to various empirical analyses. The significant amount of these studies can not least be explained by the CSR advocates' aspiration to prove that a positive social performance is not only good for ethical reasons, but that it also provides economic benefits. Management should therefore consider CSR in their decisions:

> "The development of this literature from the early days of Preston and Post (1975) up through the recent work on cause-related marketing and strategic philanthropy can be characterized by the simple idea that CSR/CSP would be supported by managers and their decision making process if only it could be shown that companies can 'do good and do well,' or even better that they can 'do well by doing good'."[61]

Efforts to support such an assumption empirically require adequate measures by means of which it is possible to quantify the underlying constructs of CSP and CFP without violating criteria of objectivity, reliability and validity. While the measures for firm financial performance have not been a reason for major dissent,[62] no consent has been achieved as to the most appropriate way to evaluate CSP. The empirical literature offers a broad range of attempts to measure firm social performance.

Therefore, an adequate way of categorising prior research on the CSP/CFP-link is to ask how the studies operationalise the construct of CSP, respectively. As regards content, some studies only consider one component of CSR, for instance by exclusively using environmental data. Others include multiple components in their proxy for CSP by measuring issues such as the environmental performance,

---

56 Again, cf. Fig. 2.1 on p. 7.

57 See Hülsmann et al. (2004); Utting (2000).

58 For an overview, see Habisch (2003); Matten and Crane (2005).

59 Wartick and Rude (1986); Wood (1991b); Wood and Jones (1995), p. 230.

60 See, e.g. Norman and MacDonald (2004).

61 Wood and Jones (1995), pp. 234–235.

62 For an overview of the most commonly used financial performance measures, see Orlitzky et al. (2003), pp. 407 et seq.; Sen and Bhattacharya (2001), p. 226[2].

		Source of Information		
		Perception-based	Performance-based	Content-Analysis
Number of Dimensions	single	personal assessment; interviews	environmental *or* social *or* philanthropic	corporate publications; media coverage
	multiple	internal/ external expert interviews	environmental *and* social *and* philanthropic	
		multi-dimensional ratings; aggregated indices; meta-analyses		

Fig. 2.4 A classification of CSP-measures

employee treatment, and charitable contributions. The empirical literature can thus be classified by looking at whether they use one- or multi-dimensional constructs as CSP-measures. With respect to the source of information, there are three categories of proxies for CSR. Especially earlier studies used perception-based measures, e.g. by asking internal or external experts to asses a given company's social performance. A second category relies on performance-based information, such as data on air pollution discharge or charitable expenditures. The last type of studies uses content-analyses of corporate and other publications to measure a firm's CSP. Figure 2.4 categorises different CSP-measures, according to which the following discussion of empirical studies is structured. This discussion does not aim at exhaustively analysing *all* studies but rather intends to offer a systematic and critical classification of approaches to measure the CSP/CFP-link.

2.2.3 *Empirical Studies on the CSP/CFP-Link: Different Measures of CSP*

2.2.3.1 Perception-Based Measures

The study from Moskowitz (1972) is commonly cited as the earliest attempt to empirically investigate the relationship between a company's efforts to adhere to its social responsibilities and its financial performance. By generally speaking of "socially responsible" corporate behaviour, and thereby considering CSP one-dimensionally, this study assumes that a socially responsible portfolio also economically performs superior. However, when choosing socially responsible corporations, the author relies on his subjective perception rather than on objective criteria:

> "It is extremely difficult to construct standards by which a company's social performance can be accurately measured (...). After four years of closely monitoring businesses' social involvement, however, I have observed a number of company names cropping up time after time with regard to positive and constructive responses to social problems."[63]

From today's perspective, this procedure surely does not satisfy scientific standards. Nevertheless, subsequent empirical studies repeatedly used Moskowitz's list but did not come to unequivocal results.[64]

A number of other authors have measured CSP multi-dimensionally by referring to the *Fortune Reputation Index*. The *Fortune Magazine* annually interviews managers and stock analysts as external experts within one industry respectively, and asks them to evaluate companies relatively to the strongest competitor and with respect to eight different criteria.[65] As one of them is *Responsibility to the Community/Environment*, this survey includes both societal as well as environmental issues. Analyses of the CSP/CFP-link have repeatedly used the referenced part of the *Fortune Reputation Index*, although this has led to mixed results.[66] Preston and O'Bannon (1997) use *Fortune* data as well, but in addition to *Community and Environmental Responsibility*, they include the two dimensions *Ability to Select and Retain Good People* and *Quality of Products and Services*. Their analysis claims a positive relation between these criteria (as a proxy for CSP) and financial success.[67] Choosing the internal perspective, Aupperle et al. (1985) follow Carroll's (1979) definition of CSR and use a forced-choice instrument to assess the attitude of firm representatives towards CSR.[68] In this case, CSP is understood as a multi-dimensional construct that includes economic, legal, ethical, and discretionary responsibilities.[69] The authors then measure the three latter dimensions' relation to the return on assets (ROA) as a proxy for CFP, but eventually fail to prove a significant correlation.[70]

The use of perception-based measures as CSP proxies has been subjected to serious criticism concerning a lack of objectivity[71] or methodological difficulties such

---

[63] Moskowitz (1972), pp. 71–72.

[64] Vance (1975) claims a negative link, Alexander and Buchholz (1978), p. 485, discover no significant results, and Cochran and Wood (1984), pp. 54 et sqq. – depending on the sample in use – find positive *and* negative relations.

[65] Cf. Wokutch and Spencer (1987), p. 66, or Fombrum and Shanley (1990), pp. 242 et seq.

[66] Spencer and Taylor (1987), p. 14, Stanwick and Stanwick (1998), p. 198 and Wokutch and Spencer (1987), pp. 70 et sqq. find a positive relation, whereas McGuire et al. (1988), pp. 865 et sqq. come to positive, non-significant, and negative results, depending on the time horizon and the measure for financial performance. For a study with similar data, cf. Luo and Bhattacharya (2006).

[67] Cf. Preston and O'Bannon (1997), pp. 426 et sqq.

[68] With this method, the respondents receive a questionnaire containing several statements, to which they have to allocate a limited amount of points depending on their level of agreement. This way, they are forced to hierarchically sort the statements according to their preferences.

[69] Cf. the discussion of Carroll's model on p. 14.

[70] Cf. Aupperle et al. (1985), p. 461.

[71] Cf. Carroll (1991a), p. 392; Cochran and Wood (1984), p. 43; Ullman (1985), p. 546; Wokutch and McKinney (1991), p. 311; Wood and Jones (1995), pp. 238 et seq.

as halo-effects[72] and multicollinearity.[73] In order to avoid this kind of criticism, some empirical studies have instead used clearly quantifiable and arguably more objective indicators such as performance-based measures of CSP.

2.2.3.2 Performance-Based Measures

Studies using purely environmental indicators form an example of one-dimensional conceptions of CSP. In this context, a common way of judging a company's CSP is the use of data provided by the *Council on Economic Priorities* (CEP).[74] The CEP used to publish rankings on the environmental pollution discharge of multinational corporations within different industries.[75] These rankings can build the basis for indices which can then serve as a measure of CSP. Using this approach, some studies find a positive relation between this measure and indicators of profitability,[76] whereas others only come to non-significant[77] or ambiguous[78] results. Also falling into the category of one-dimensional measures are those efforts that measure CSP by looking at corporate charitable donations. Not surprisingly, these studies result in the claim of a positive CSP/CFP-Link,[79] which is plausible since financially well-operating companies are especially able to afford such expenditures.

Finally, there exist approaches that combine multiple dimensions for performance-based measures of CSP. Lerner and Fryxell (1988) for instance do not restrict their analysis to CEP data but additionally include charitable expenditures and the shares of both women and minorities on the board of directors and in top management positions. Their results vary, depending on the component of CSP considered. In a similar way, Diltz (1995, with ambiguous results) and Roberts (1992, who claims a positive link) use the multi-dimensional CEP ratings developed later in time.[80]

---

[72] Cf. Brown and Perry (1994).

[73] Cf. Wood (1995), p. 198.

[74] Examples of studies that also exclusively consider the environmental dimension – although with different data than those from the CEP – are Christmann (2000); Hart and Ahuja (1996); Klassen and McLaughlin (1996); Klassen and Whybark (1999); Konar and Cohen (2001). All of these studies discover a positive relation of their environmental indicators with financial measures.

[75] Cf. Spicer (1978a), pp. 101 et seq. Later, the CEP also published comprehensive, multi-dimensional rankings, cf. Diltz (1995), p. 71.

[76] Cf. Bragdon and Marlin (1972); Shane and Spicer (1983); Spicer (1978a).

[77] Cf. Chen and Metcalf (1980) or Freedman and Jaggi (1982).

[78] Cf. Pava and Krausz (1996).

[79] Cf. Fry et al. (1982); Galaskiewicz (1997); Levy and Shatto (1980); Maddox and Siegfried (1980).

[80] Cf. footnote 86.

2.2.3.3 Content Analyses

Besides perception-based and performance-based measures, content analyses of corporate and other publications build a third way of operationalising the construct of CSP. Most important in this context are companies' annual reports, but studies using this technique of analysis also consider employee manuals, corporate magazines, speeches of managers, SEC 10-Ks or media reports. Within this category, different one-dimensional approaches can be identified.

One of the earliest of such studies, exclusively considering the social dimension, can be found at Bowman and Haire (1975), who conduct a purely quantitative analysis but totally abstain from differentiating with regards to content:

> "In searching for a readily available surrogate measure for actual activities in the area of corporate citizenship, we chose to measure the proportion of lines of prose in the annual report devoted to social responsibility".[81]

Since this rather pragmatic approach, the technique of content analysis has become refined,[82] but nevertheless has not been widely used anymore in recent empirical studies.[83] Besides social issues, certain studies have only considered the environmental information in corporate publications. However, most of these studies only produced insignificant results.[84]

Interestingly, no multi-dimensional content analyses have been used for investigations into the CSP/CFP-link, despite the existence of surveys and even ratings based on CSR reports.[85] This is partly due to the rise of alternative, more comprehensive and reliable measures of CSP which are generated by professional raters.

2.2.3.4 Comprehensive Multidimensional Measures and Aggregated Indices

Especially in recent studies, the use of data provided by professional rating agencies such as *Kinder, Lydenberg, Domini & Co.* (KLD) forms a widely-used way of measuring a firm's social performance.[86] KLD developed a rating system for

---

[81] Bowman and Haire (1975), pp. 49 et seq. This study does not come to unambiguous results as to the CSP and CFP-link.

[82] Cf. Wolfe (1991), pp. 291 et sqq.

[83] For studies using content analyses – though discovering different results as to the CSP/CFP-link – see Abbott and Monsen (1979); Anderson and Frankle (1980); Fry and Hock (1976); and Preston (1978).

[84] Cf. Freedman and Jaggi (1986) and Ingram and Frazier (1983). Blacconiere and Patten (1994), pp. 374 et sqq., however, who additionally consider investments into "green" technology, claim a significant and positive link.

[85] Cf. KPMG Global Sustainability Services (2005) or Kirchhoff (2007).

[86] Waddock (2003), p. 369, calls the use of KLD-data the *"de facto* research standard at the moment". For a critique of this approach see Entine (2003) and Jarvis et al. (2003). For a deeper discussion of KLD's methodology, see Sect. 3.1.1.2. Concerning the use of different but similar multi-dimensional ratings drawing (amongst others) on CEP data, see Diltz (1995); Roberts (1992). For a comprehensive discussion of various rating agencies and their screening methodologies, see Schäfer et al. (2006).

the assessment of CSP. The rating's results are used to decide upon exclusion and inclusion of corporations in sustainability indices such as the *Domini Social Index* 400, or sold to Socially Responsible Investment (SRI) fund managers. KLD assesses companies along the various components such as *Community Relations, Employee Relations, Environment, Women and Minority Issues, Product Liability, Tobacco/Gambling/Alcohol, Military Contracting/Nuclear Power* and *South African Involvement*.[87] Within this group of empirical studies, one can further distinguish two kinds of investigations. Some test the statistical influence of single component on financial measures. Others use all components to build an aggregated index and then scrutinise its link to CFP measures.

The studies of Berman et al. (1999) and Graves and Waddock (2000) are examples of isolated analyses of the respective components' effects on CFP. Both eventually come to the conclusion that a positive CSP/CFP-link exists (which – put this way – is an undifferentiated claim again). However, a number of other studies also used KLD data but only lead to non-significant[88] or – depending on the dimension in use – ambiguous[89] results. Similarly, Glaser et al. (2007) perform isolated correlation analyses between single CSP components and different measures of financial performance. The authors mainly find significant correlations between employees-related sub-ratings and financial accounting numbers. For their study, Glaser et al. (2007) draw on data from *oekom research*, a German corporate responsibility rating agency similar to KLD. Since these data will also be used in the empirical analysis later, Sect. 3.1.1.3 will critically review the methodology of the Glaser et al. (2007) study.

Ruf et al. (2001), p. 148, criticise that an equal consideration of each of the KLD dimensions overestimates the importance of certain criteria and therefore causes a bias in favour of less important aspects. Thus, they first interview experts on the importance of each component, then weight each category according to their responses and finally aggregate them into a cumulated index.[90] As a result of the subsequent regression analysis, they find a positive correlation between the index scores and different accounting-based financial indicators. Graves and Waddock (1994) use the same method for measuring CSP. They discover a positive link between a company's CSP and its attractiveness for institutional investors, but fail to prove positive results as to its relation with market-based and accounting-based CFP measures. Waddock and Graves (1997), however, use the identical procedure and confirm their hypotheses that there is a positive and significant influence of

[87] For a description, see Sharfman (1996), pp. 288 et seq. and Graves and Waddock (1994:1098). Later, KLD rated along ten dimensions, see Waddock (2000), p. 30 and even 12 dimensions, cf. Mattingly and Berman (2006), p. 29. Since assessments take place on the basis of both surveys as well as third party information (media, etc.), all three sources of data referred to above (see Fig. 2.4) are included in this CSP-measure.

[88] Cf. Guerard (1997); Kurtz and DiBartolomeo (1996); McWilliams and Siegel (2000).

[89] Cf. Graves and Waddock (1994); Hillman and Keim (2001); Johnson and Greening (1999).

[90] Each company's score is then calculated according to the formula $CSP_i = \sum w_j \times a_{ij}$. For an in-depth description of the procedure concerning the weighting factors w_j, cf. Ruf et al. (1998).

CSP on CFP and *vice versa*.[91] Another way of aggregating several indices into one score can be found at Griffin and Mahon (1997). The authors take four different indices,[92] built an average rank for each company, and thereby form a comprehensive index. They then measure this CSP proxy against five different indicators of financial performance, with mostly positive results.

Similar to the direct use of data from rating agencies for correlation analyses are performance studies of socially-screened investment funds and indices. As the latter are constructed on the basis of data from rating agencies such as KLD, they principally correspond to the hitherto mentioned studies. However, they do differ with respect to the CFP measure, as they compare the funds' and indices' stock market performance to that of conventional portfolios. As a result of his review of such studies, Schröder (2004) concludes that socially-screened funds and indices generally do not significantly differ from conventional ones in their economic performance. These findings are in accordance with his "own performance analyses [which] show that most of the German, Swiss and U.S. SRI investment funds do not significantly underperform their benchmarks."[93]

2.2.3.5 Meta-Analyses

As a reaction to the fact that previous research into the CSP/CFP-link had not succeeded in coming to clear results, efforts emerged to analyse already existing investigations and in this way to draw generalisable conclusions. Several narrative meta-analyses try to resort previous studies, find explanations for their mixed results, and reorient future research.[94] In contrast, Orlitzky et al. (2003) conducted a quantitative meta-analysis. In this study, the authors start with the assumption that differences in empirical results concerning the CSP/CFP-link are traceable mainly to differences in measuring social and financial performance. Hence, referring to the quantitative meta-analysis technique proposed by Hunter and Schmidt (1990), they try to identify the "true score correlation" of each study, that is, correlations that are cleared up from influences of differences in samples and in measurement strategies. As a result, they find support for their hypothesis and conclude that "there is a positive association between CSP and CFP across industries and across study contexts."[95]

---

[91] In order to test the influence of financial performance on CSP, Waddock and Graves (1997), pp. 310 et seq. once use financial measures as independent variables and CSP as the dependent variable (and the other way around to test CSP's influence on financial performance).

[92] They use an index built from KLD data, the Fortune Reputation Index, the Toxic Release Inventory Index and a rank based on corporate charitable donations. Cf. Griffin and Mahon (1997), pp. 14 et sqq.

[93] Schröder (2004), p. 131. For another overview with the same conclusion, cf. Schäfer and Stederoth (2002), p. 129.

[94] See for instance Allouche and Laroche (2005); Bakker et al. (2005); Margolis and Walsh (2003); Pava and Krausz (1996); Preston and O'Bannon (1997); Roman et al. (1999).

[95] Orlitzky et al. (2003), p. 423.

As the analysis of selected empirical studies has shown, research into the CSP/CFP-link has so far failed to provide a homogenous picture, let alone unanimous results. The following chapter offers an explanatory analysis of this and draws conclusions that lay the grounds for the empirical analysis, which will follow in the course of this thesis.

2.3 A Framework for an Empirical Analysis of CSP

Based on the critique of earlier empirical studies, the following will argue that an examination of the CSP/CFP-link has to take place in a methodologically refined way. First, for the purpose of analysing such a link, it is of no use to employ aggregated measures of a company's social performance in a comprehensive sense, but it is appropriate to clearly separate single components of social performance and their respective relation to CFP (2.2.3.1). Second, before performing a statistical test of such a relation, it is advisable to ask what determinants might influence the level of CSR engagement at all (2.2.3.2). Finally, instead of looking for a universal link, a differentiated statistical analysis should ask why and under what conditions a certain link should exist. It is proposed that these questions can be taken into account by including moderating (2.2.3.3.) as well as mediating effects (2.2.3.4.) into the analysis. Figure 2.5 depicts the structure of the following:

2.3.1 Decomposing the Construct of CSP

Considering the fact that the studies reviewed above use so many different ways of operationalising the construct of CSP, other than ambiguous results as to the

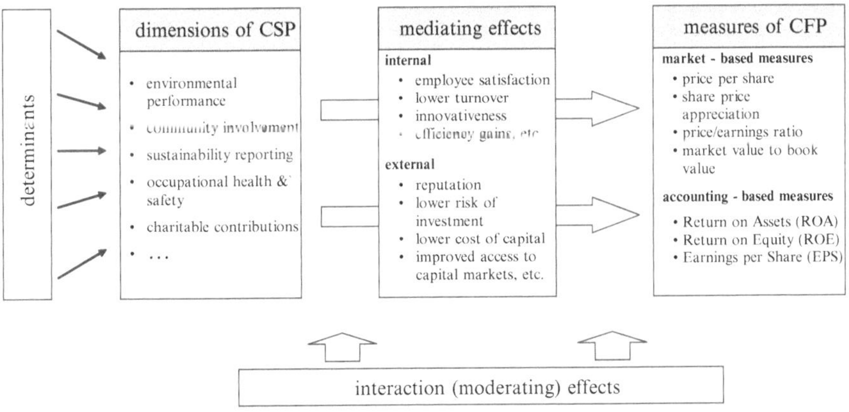

Fig. 2.5 A frame of reference for analysing the CSP/CFP-link

CSP/CFP-link would have been surprising. The number of lines in annual reports devoted to social issues for instance, and the amount of charitable donations, do not reflect the same construct. Therefore, claiming that these very different measures would reflect the same phenomenon, namely CSP, eventually denies the construct's inherently multidimensional nature[96] and renders the respective results incomparable. Even if the studies turned out to provide clear results, it would be impossible to interpret them. If, say, superior environmental performance and above-average philanthropic donations both proved to be beneficial for firm profitability, this would most probably be traceable to different reasons, which cannot be treated under the same term. This criticism especially applies to aggregated indices and quantitative meta-analyses that treat different studies as if they investigated the same facts. Looking for *the* ultimate CSP/CFP-link means treating different studies under the same label; this leaves no room for differentiation and leads to a loss of information. Eventually, with such a procedure, it cannot be said whether a strong correlation is due to a high environmental performance, good employee treatment, excellent community relations, or a superior corporate reputation. Correlation analyses should therefore only measure single CSP components' effects on a company's financial performance, instead of asking for the overall relation of CSP and CFP.[97] This would then lead to a more differentiated analysis than questions of the type "do socially responsible companies generally perform better?".

The problem then remains, how these single components could be identified. For the purpose of this paper, considering the difficulties to clearly define CSR and separate ethical from economic or legal issues, an identification of these dimensions has to rely on other criteria than those offered by common CSR definitions. Drawing on the results of Sect. 2.1, CSR issues can be distinguished by using instrumental aspects of the stakeholder concept and asking which stakeholders ascribe responsibilities to companies. Such an approach has of course certain implications for the definition of CSR. It understands CSR as the sum of responsibilities ascribed by various stakeholders due to their perceived value conflicts.

As already mentioned, this means that the concrete contents of the concept can vary according to the values holding for a given society at a certain point in time. If, for example, the companies' *social* responsibility were perceived to be identical with its duty to gain profits,[98] CSP would not need to be measured as an own construct. If, however, stakeholders *do* ascribe responsibilities other than purely economic ones to companies, the measurement of CSP has to include other dimensions such as environmental performance, relations to the community, working standards, etc. Given such an understanding, the measurement of CSP has to narrow down its research aim: Instead of asking what impact CSP (as one all-comprising, clearly

---

[96] Cf. point (4) on p. 18.

[97] In this respect, Rowley and Berman (2000) rightly argue that CSP should be used as a comprehensive *brand* for a topic of research, rather than as the label for one theoretical or operational construct. In the following – in spite of the suggestion to separately measure single components' effects on CFP – the undifferentiated terms "CSP" and "CSP/CFP-link" will still be used for the sake of simplicity.

[98] Cf. the cited literature in footnote 5.

defined concept) altogether *does* have, it is appropriate to ask what effects *single components* of CSP *can* have.

2.3.2 Explaining CSP: When can Superior Social Performance be Expected?

A second point addresses the probability of good social performance itself by scrutinising the so far widely neglected question, under which conditions a strong CSP can be expected at all. Before asking whether and what kind of a link exists between components of CSP and CFP, one should first analyse under what circumstances CSP might be important to companies. For instance, it would be counterintuitive to assume that privately owned mid-size firms in B2B industries have the same interests to pursue CSR strategies as highly visible, publicly traded producers of consumer goods. Identifying the main determinants of CSP is of specific relevance for the research aim of this thesis, because the indication of systematic reasons for companies to have CSR on their agenda might allow for initial conclusions as to the hypotheses concerning the CSP/CFP-link.

The search for determinants of CSP implies the question *why* companies should have an increased interest to perform well along a certain dimension of CSR. In an approach to address this question normatively (*should* companies admit social responsibilities?), recent efforts have tried to understand CSP by attributing a new political role to business in today's societies and also assuming a changed self-perception of companies.[99] A positive analysis of the question why companies actually *do* pursue CSR strategies can, however, as well manage without the assumption of a new societal role of business. This would then mean to interpret CSP as a mere market response which can be put down to the firm's profit-maximizing calculus. This implies that assumptions as to the corporate rationale to pursue such strategies are held constant, and the focus of analysis shifts to changes in societal demands directed to the company. CSR engagement, including the implementation of organisational structures and management tools, is then interpreted as the effort to seek legitimacy by adhering to new environmental expectations rather than to changing internal requirements.[100] To put it differently, the company's assumed social responsibilities are merely a "parameter of action",[101] that is, just another restriction that has to be taken into account within the firm's economic rationality.[102]

---

[99] Cf. for instance Palazzo and Scherer (2006). See also the discussion in Utting (2000), p. 9 et sqq., whether one can rightly assume a "paradigm shift" in business.

[100] Cf. Meyer and Rowan (1991); Scott (1995), pp. 66 et sqq.; Süß and Kleiner (2006), pp. 526 et sqq.; Walgenbach and Beck (2003), pp. 498 et sqq.; see also Sect. 2.1.2.1.

[101] Picot (1977), p. 37 (my translation).

[102] Such a positive analysis can of course be used for prescriptive propositions, which then leads to instrumental and finally normative theory. For such a normative managerial CSR approach, see McWilliams and Siegel (2001).

From such a perspective, it is unlikely that all companies evenly pursue CSP under all circumstances, because external expectations to companies generally vary according to determinants such as the industry, product characteristics, or firm size, to name just a few. Therefore, an empirical investigation of CSP's economic effects first has to analyse in which cases companies (do not) have an incentive to pursue certain CSR strategies. Such an analysis is of a crucial importance for subsequently deriving hypotheses concerning the CSP/CFP-link. Examples of such determinants include the owner structure of the company, the degree to which respective industries are unionised, possible shortages of skilled workers, firm size and diversification, industry and company visibility.[103] Although not all of these determinants can be taken into account in this study, Sect. 3.2 presents an empirical analysis of selected drivers of CSP. It does so by asking which factors help predicting good or bad performance with respect to certain aspects of CSP.

2.3.3 Interaction Effects: Under What Conditions Should a Link to Financial Performance Exist?

Besides identifying determinants that influence the extent of CSP itself, an analysis also has to clarify, which parameters might influence its link to financial performance. Assuming an unconditioned relation between respective measures for social and financial performance would mean to deny both that socially irresponsible behaviour does pay in certain cases and that in other cases, beyond-compliance behaviour can turn out to be very costly without being outbalanced by future returns.[104] In econometrics, parameters that can influence the strengths and direction of the relation between two other variables are called interaction effects. Such effects are sometimes also called moderator effects because the interacting third variable which changes the relation between two original variables is a variable that moderates the original relationship.[105] An empirical investigation of the CSP/CFP-link thus has to take into account interaction effects which help explain under which circumstances such a link might exist.

Hence, instead of empirically testing the existence of a universal link between (components of) CSP and financial indicators, it might be useful to apply a contingency approach. This allows for an analysis of the conditions, under which strong CSP comes along with superior economic performance, or, on the contrary,

---

[103] Cf. McWilliams and Siegel (2001); Thompson and Smith (1991), p. 31; Ullman (1985).

[104] The fact that the business case argument is not self-evident becomes clear through the statement of a businessman quoted in Utting (2000), p. 21: "If the 'win-win' argument were so compelling (i.e. if there were such scope for simultaneously making profits and improving a company's social and environmental performance), then we wouldn't be sitting around this table." For studies that (contra-intuitively) identify *adverse* effects of a company's CSR efforts on potential customers' evaluation of the firm, see Schwaiger (2004) or Sen and Bhattacharya (2001).

[105] Cf. Hair et al. (2006), pp. 201 et sqq.

with financial losses. The resource-based view of the firm offers a useful frame of reference for such a conceptual analysis, as it helps explain under which (external) conditions (internal) resources or "core competencies"[106] can be turned into a competitive advantage.[107] By definition,

> "...*firm resources* include all assets, capabilities, organizational processes, firm attributes, information, knowledge, etc. controlled by a firm that enable the firm to conceive of and implement strategies that improve its efficiency and effectiveness."[108]

Not all resources, however, lead to competitive advantages. In order to hold the potential of providing competitive advantages to the respective firm, resources have to display certain characteristics: They have to (a) be able to exploit opportunities and/or neutralise threats in a firm's environment; (b) be either tacit, socially complex or rare among a firm's competitors; (c) be imperfectly imitable; and (d) have no substitutes that fulfil the first three conditions.[109]

Applied to the context of this study, the ability to exploit opportunities by implementing CSR strategies can be seen as a firm's (internal) resource that it can, under certain (external) circumstances, turn into a valuable asset.[110] In the course of the following, it will therefore be necessary to first identify such conditions and test their moderating effects on the link to CFP by including them into the empirical analysis.

Earlier conceptual and empirical work on the CSP/CFP-link already offers several suggestions for potential moderators that help bring together internal capabilities and external conditions – however often without offering ways to statistically operationalise these moderators. Examples include management's strategic posture towards environmental[111] or social[112] demands; industry growth[113] and visibility[114]; a firm's capability for process innovation and implementation[115]; consumers' attitude to CSR and their beliefs about the relation between a company's CSR efforts

---

[106] Prahalad and Hamel (1990).

[107] See for instance Barney (1991), p. 102; Conner (1991), p. 122; Grant (1991), p. 118; Hart (1995), p. 988; Russo and Fouts (1997), pp. 536 et sqq.; Wernerfelt (1984), p. 172. For a strategic management approach to CSR, see Porter and Kramer (2006).

[108] Barney (1991), p. 101 (italics in original).

[109] Cf. Barney (1991), pp. 105 et seq.; Hart (1995), pp. 989 and 998.

[110] Cf. Hart (1995); Russo and Fouts (1997) that understand environmental performance as a corporate resource. Concerning CSR and the resources-based perspective, see Branco and Rodriguez (2006) and the literature cited there.

[111] Cf. Wagner and Schaltegger (2004), pp. 559 and 562. Considering the said above, it is critical to assume strategy to moderate the CSP/CFP-link, though. Understanding CSR as a market response, strategy should rather be seen as a function of its importance: professional CSR management can only be expected where external pressure asks for it and where it therefore pays to have one (see also Sect. 2.3.2).

[112] Cf. Ullman (1985), pp. 551 et seq.

[113] Cf. Russo and Fouts (1997), pp. 540 et sqq.

[114] Cf. Ullman (1985), p. 542.

[115] Cf. Christmann (2000), p. 669.

and its ability to make quality products[116]; stakeholder power[117] and their ability to engage in networks[118]; country-specific regulatory differences or industry market structure[119]; and managerial orientation towards stakeholders.[120]

Understanding CSR as a market response, a positive CSP/CFP-link is more likely to exist in those instances where the company has an interest to intensify its CSR efforts. In other cases, however, increased CSP can even lead to an economic underperformance: if a company spends more resources for CSR without expecting respective returns, it will – *ceteris paribus* – be less profitable than a comparable competitor. This example illustrates the close interrelations between determinants of CSP and moderators of the CSP/CFP-link. Despite these similarities it is important to note that, in the terminology used in the following, determinants and moderators are conceptually different: while determinants influence the CSP level itself, moderators influence its link to financial performance. If CSP can be considered as a rational market response,[121] variables that prove to increase the probability of a high/low CSP are most likely to have a moderating effect on the CSP/CFP-link. Due to technical restrictions, not all of the conceivable interaction effects can be employed in the empirical study presented later. To focus on the most important ones, Sect. 3.2 examines potential drivers (determinants) of a high CSP and will thereby identify the most promising candidates for interaction effects employed in Sect. 3.3.

As mentioned earlier, identifying moderators means asking under which conditions a certain relation might exist. Additionally, one can assume that if such a link exists, it does not do so to an unlimited extent. In the contrary, there presumably is a level of CSR efforts where the company meets societal expectations to a satisfying degree.[122] Arguably, the marginal utility of additional such efforts will turn negative from that point on. By depicting the relation between CSP and economic performance as an inverted u-shaped curve, researchers have repeatedly formalised this assumption.[123] However, empirical studies on the CSP/CFP-link have seldom used a function of such a type.[124] Section 3.5 will address the idea of decreasing marginal net benefits from investments into CSP and present a possibility to statistically test the empirical validity of this assumption.

---

116 Cf. Sen and Bhattacharya (2001), p. 227.

117 Cf. Mitchell et al. (1997), p. 878; Barnett (2007).

118 Cf. Rowley (1997).

119 Cf. Wagner and Wehrmeyer (2002), p. 137.

120 Cf. Berman et al. (1999), p. 492.

121 Cf. pp. 32 et sqq.

122 See McWilliams and Siegel (2001), who conclude that form a managerial perspective there is an "ideal level of CSR".

123 Bowman (1973), p. 25; Picot (1977), p. 33; Schaltegger and Synnestvedt (2002), p. 341; Ullman (1985), p. 542; Wagner et al. (2002), p. 135; Wagner and Schaltegger (2004), p. 558. For a visualisation of this idea, cf. Fig. 2.12 on p. 92 of this thesis.

124 For an effort to take into account decreasing marginal returns of CSP when measuring its relation to economic performance, see Bowman and Haire (1975).

2.3.4 Mediating Effects: Why Should a CSP/CFP-Link Exist?

Statistical tests of empirical correlations first require conceptually derived hypotheses concerning these interrelations.[125] In the case of economic impacts of corporate social performance, such predictions have to be based on theoretically deducted arguments on why the performance on a certain component of CSP should have financial effects for a given company.[126] Hence, another argument starts with the observation that there is no reason for the existence of a (causal) relationship between CSP and CFP unless one takes into consideration certain mechanisms that provide an explanation for why such a link should exist. That is, when asking for such an explanation, one has to look for mediating effects. The ability to sustain higher margins due to a better customer reputation on the one hand, and having higher employee satisfaction which leads to better productivity on the other hand, both might have positive impacts on a firm's financial performance, but through very different and distinct mechanisms. Clearly distinguishing between these different mechanisms is not only important for methodological reasons but also for management that has to base its CSR related (investment) decisions on a profound understanding of their consequences. A first approach to identifying mediators lies within the distinction between organisationally internal and external effects of CSP.

Mediators reflecting internal effects consider advantages that the organisation can achieve through CSP internally and that lead to economically relevant benefits. This first of all applies to the firm's employees, who may support the company's CSR activities and therefore perceive increased satisfaction and identification with their jobs, which in turn can result in lowered absenteeism and turnover.[127] This identification effect can furthermore enhance a given company's ability to attract qualified employees.[128] Concerning the production processes within the firm, especially environmental management and related process improvements can help the company develop competencies that lead to more efficient work processes[129] and enhanced innovativeness.[130] Furthermore, eco-oriented management might be better prepared for anticipating and handling risks.[131]

A company's social performance does not only have an impact on management and employees but is also observed by stakeholders outside the firm. That makes it plausible to assume that CSP causes certain external effects. Arguably most intensively researched in this context are reputational effects of CSR efforts. In the broadest sense, CSP can be seen as a means to ensure a company's legitimacy

[125] Cf. Backhaus et al. (2006), p. 7.

[126] See Ullman (1985), pp. 551 et sqq.; Wood and Jones (1995), pp. 230 et sqq.; Rowley and Berman (2000), p. 405.

[127] Cf. Berman et al. (1999), pp. 489 et seq.; Clarkson (1995), p. 93; Maignan et al. (1999), p. 459; Riordan et al. (1997); Wagner and Schaltegger (2004), p. 564.

[128] Cf. Turban and Greening (1997).

[129] Cf. Hamschmidt and Dyllick (2001); Hart (1995), pp. 998 et sqq.

[130] Cf. McWilliams and Siegel (2000), pp. 605 et seq.

[131] Cf. Shrivastava (1995).

within society, or as it is sometimes called, its "license to operate".[132] More detailed, empirical investigations have found that perceived CSP in general, and particularly environmental performance,[133] has – mostly positive – effects on a firm's overall reputation.[134] Such superior reputation is an important corporate asset as it influences consumer behaviour[135] and enables companies to add price premiums on their products.[136] CSP might also come along with financially benign effects on capital markets. It can for instance lower a company's capital costs (as socially responsible firms tend to be less risky investments[137]) and enable access to certain new capital markets.[138]

Given the existence of such potential internal and external mediating effects, an empirical investigation of the CSP/CFP-link first has to analyse which components of CSP might have an influence on these mediators. This will be accomplished in Sect. 3.3.1 which thoroughly derives hypotheses as to the single components' effects on firm financial performance.

---

[132] Cf. Hansen and Schrader (2005), p. 384; Hart (1995), p. 999.

[133] Cf. Hart (1995), p. 999; Russo and Fouts (1997), p. 539.

[134] See for instance Eberl and Schwaiger (2006); Hansen and Schrader (2005), pp. 383 et seq.; Schwaiger (2004); Sen and Bhattacharya (2001), p. 226.

[135] Cf. Maignan et al. (1999), p. 459; Mohr et al. (2001); Sen and Bhattacharya (2001).

[136] Cf. McWilliams and Siegel (2001), p. 119.

[137] Cf. Graves and Waddock (1994), pp. 1043 et seq.; Fombrum et al. (2000); Spicer (1978b, pp. 75 et sqq.; Wagner and Schaltegger (2004), p. 564.

[138] This argument refers to capital markets associated with *Socially Responsible Investment* (SRI). For a recent overview, see Schröder (2004).

Chapter 3
An Empirical Study on Corporate Social Performance

The empirical analysis of economic impacts of corporate social performance in this second main section of the thesis proceeds in five steps. The first task is to present the data employed in this study. Section 3.1 will therefore include a qualitative as well as a quantitative examination of the CSP data derived from *oekom research* ratings. It will also justify the argument that *oekom* data are more adequate for empirical CSR research than previously used data, and that the only existing study that employs *oekom* data still leaves many questions unanswered. Moreover, it provides a discussion and descriptive statistics of all financial data and control variables used. Particularly, it will give reasons for the use of *Tobin's Q* as a market-based measure of financial performance.

Second, to better understand what kind of companies tend to display a good CSP, Sect. 3.2 will analyse the influence of potential CSP drivers. After considering CSP at an aggregated level, the two sub-categories of that rating (social-cultural and environmental rating) will be scrutinised separately to see whether results change in a more differentiated kind of analysis. The results of that section will partly be used to identify possible interaction effects included in the subsequent analysis in Sect. 3.3. After deriving hypotheses as to the relation between five CSP components and *Tobin's Q*, these will be tested by cross-sectional regression analyses. The then following robustness check of the model will address the econometric problem of endogeneity, which is often involved in the context of regression analyses. Specifically, by means of an instrumental variable regression, it will ask to which degree the results allow for conclusions as to the causal relations between CSP and financial performance.

Section 3.4 asks whether there is a relation between changes in the performance along CSP components and *Tobin's Q*, respectively. Although no entire panel dataset is available, a dynamic analysis of the data is possible by using a sub-set of the sample for which observations are available for two points in time.

Finally, Sect. 3.5 will examine the aforementioned idea that even if a positive relation between CSP components and financial performance exists, this relation might not persist to an unlimited extent. To test this hypothesis of decreasing marginal effects of CSP, it will analyse whether exceptionally good CSP comes along with financial losses.

P. Schreck, *The Business Case for Corporate Social Responsibility*,
Contributions to Management Science.

3.1 Sample Description

3.1.1 Data on Corporate Social Performance

3.1.1.1 Oekom Research's Rating Approach

The subsequent study uses data gathered and provided by *oekom research AG*, one of Germany's largest social investment research firms. *oekom research* is an independent rating agency that evaluates the social-cultural and environmental performance of publicly traded companies as well as of entire countries.[1] Their research results form the basis of their so-called *Corporate Responsibility Ratings* (CRR) and the *Country Ratings*,[2] which institutional investors use to construct their investment portfolios. These institutions are mainly socially responsible investment funds that seek to base their investment decisions on more than merely financial considerations.[3] In 1994, *oekom research* started evaluating companies on purely environmental criteria, which were supplemented by social dimensions in 1999. Since then, *oekom research* regularly publishes its industry-specific corporate responsibility ratings. Currently, its research includes more than 800 companies from various countries and all major industries; the stocks analysed cover 100% of DJ STOXX 50 and DJ EURO STOXX 50 indices, 90% of DJ STOXX 600 and 80% of the MSCI World Index. Considering the conceptualisation of CSR developed earlier, it is appropriate to use these data to assess a company's CSP, as it is based on research considering firm performance towards various stakeholders. Since investors who try to identify socially responsible companies demand these ratings, they should reflect values holding within society, upon which social responsibilities are ascribed to companies.

The agency's rating process is characterised by a comprehensive indicator-based approach. The *Frankfurt-Hohenheimer-Guidelines*, a set of more than 800 criteria for the ethical assessment of companies, serves as a blueprint for industry-specific catalogues of up to 200 single items which the companies are judged upon.[4] The grading on each of these criteria takes place on a scale ranging from A+ (excellent record) to D− (poor record), equalling a 13 steps numerical scale (grades 1–4 in 0.25 steps). To minimise method biases, professional analysts are grouped by industry experts. For the assessment of the companies, they use a highly standardised procedure and take into account quantitative measures whenever possible.

[1] For the following, cf. Bönning (2004) and the company description on www. http://www.oekom-research.com/ag/english/index_services.htm. For a comprehensive international overview of such rating institutions, see Schäfer et al. (2006).

[2] The country ratings comprise 45 OECD countries but are not further described here, as they are not subject to this paper.

[3] For an international overview of such funds and their performance cf. Schröder (2004). For a critical examination see the debate between Entine (2003) and Waddock (2003).

[4] The *Frankfurt-Hohenheimer-Guidelines* were developed and published in 1997 by the project group *Ethical & Environmental Rating*, lead by Johannes Hoffmann and Gerhard Scherhorn. Cf. Hoffmann et al. (1997); Frankfurt-Hohenheim and oekom research AG (2002).

The information for the evaluation is derived from both the companies themselves and the external sources. Company information comprises annual, social and environmental reports as well as personal interviews with company representatives. Additional information is gathered from media screening, expert interviews and assessments from specialists in governmental institutions and various organisations such as business associations, research institutes, consumer protection groups and other NGOs. Referring to the distinction introduced in Sect. 2.2.2, *oekom research* provides multi-dimensional, performance-based measures of CSP.[5]

Upon completion of the rating process, the single item grades are weighted according to an industry-specific scheme and aggregated on up to seven levels. This procedure finally results in the *Corporate Responsibility Rating*, consisting of a social and an environmental dimension, as depicted in Fig. 3.1.

Investment recommendations are given on the basis of these ratings' results. As *oekom research* follows a best-in-class approach, prerequisites for being rated as 'prime investment' vary between industries. Depending on the environmental and social impact of a given industry, the company needs to reach a minimum grade in order to be assigned the 'prime' status, that is to be recommended to investors. For instance, a company in the metals and mining industry has a relatively high environmental and social-cultural impact, which requires comparably high efforts to reduce these negative externalities. Therefore, such a company would need an over-all rating grade of at least 'B-' to be recommended to investors as 'prime'. A software company, on the other hand, would only need a minimum grade of 'C-' within the *oekom* rating to reach the same status. Note that according to this approach,

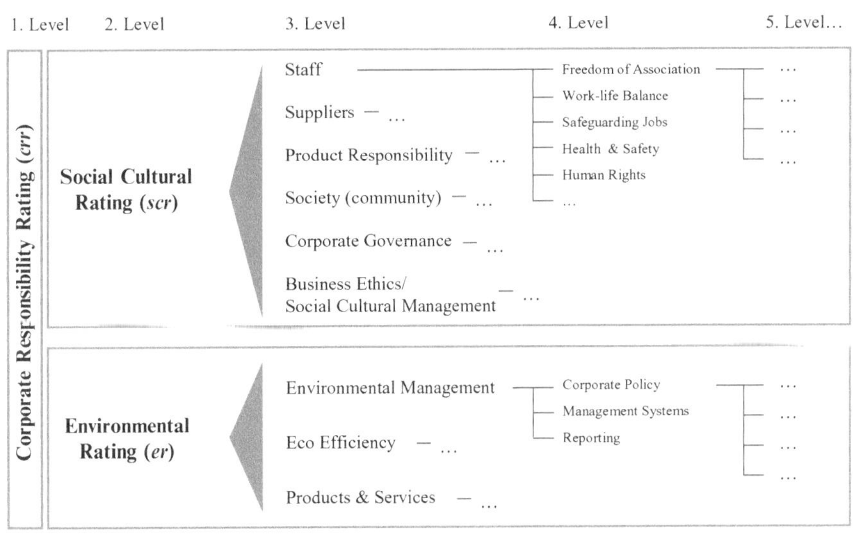

Fig. 3.1 Structure of *oekom research*'s Corporate Responsibility Rating

[5] For a better understanding, recent exemplary *oekom research* company ratings can be downloaded at the 'ratings & assessments' section on www.oekom-research.com.

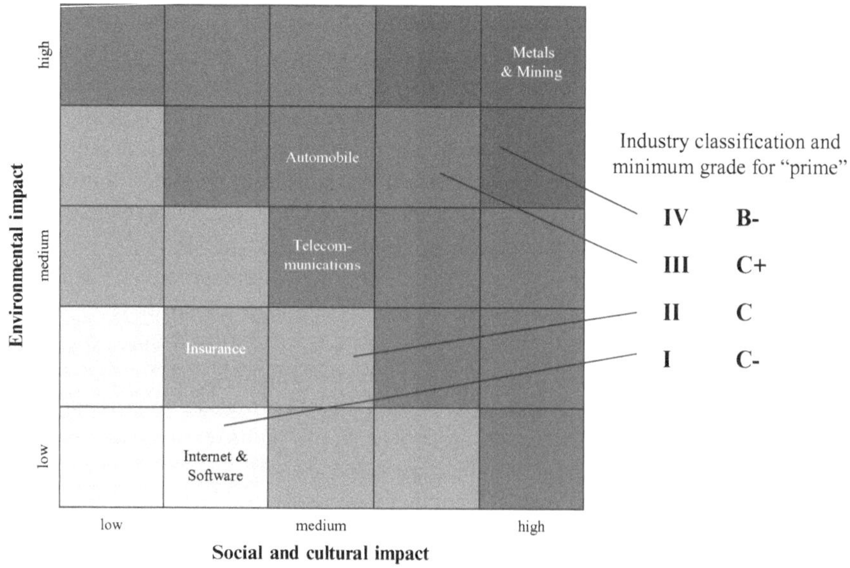

Fig. 3.2 Industry classification and minimum grades for prime status

companies are assessed on their absolute social-cultural and environmental impact first of all, and are then evaluated in relation to their industry-specific competitors. This procedure differs from other rating methodologies, a point which the examination of an alternative approach will come back to in the next chapter. The linkage between industry classification and the respective requirements for the status of a prime investment is illustrated in Fig. 3.2.[6]

oekom research tries to involve the companies within the rating process at various stages. First, firms are informed about the fact that they are being rated so that they can provide more than the publicly available information. After first completion of preliminary ratings, companies have two further opportunities to provide feedback and comments on previous ratings. The final results are published in *oekom research*'s industry reports that can be obtained by its customers.[7]

In addition to these ratings, investors who obtain data from *oekom research* can also screen out companies on the basis of various exclusionary criteria independent of the rating result. These criteria concern the company's involvement in controversial business areas (e.g. military, gambling or pornography) or practices (e.g. animal testing, violation of human rights or controversial environmental behaviour). As these form binary data, which are only used for negative screening strategies independent of the overall grade, these will not be considered in the following.

[6] Source*: oekom research AG.* Reprinted with kind permission.

[7] Taken together, the research process is so thorough and time-consuming that it takes up to six months to complete an entire industry report. Therefore, industry reports usually are only published every 3–4 years.

3.1.1.2 Comparison to KLD Data

As shown in Sect. 2.2.3.4, numerous similar analyses have already been conducted with data provided by the US-American CSR rating agency *Kinder, Lydenberg & Domini* (KLD). Most of these studies have condensed these data to aggregated measures of CSP.[8] Others have, in line with the earlier argumentation, analysed singular dimensions of CSR.[9] Regardless of methodological differences to these studies, the justification of further analyses based on *oekom* data is also grounded on the argument that data from *oekom research* might be more suitable for assessing statistically useful differences in CSP. To show this, KLD's research methodology is evaluated in the following.

In its environmental, social and governance ratings, KLD evaluates companies within a total of 12 issue-areas, as depicted in Fig. 3.3.[10] In each of these categories, a company is rated concerning certain strengths as well as weaknesses. Dichotomous variables indicate the presence ('1') or absence ('0') of certain strengths or weaknesses.[11] Additionally, the controversial business involvement rating assesses companies as to their involvement in nine different business areas.[12]

KLD's annual industry ratings are accessible via the agency's commercial online database called SOCRATES. Many researches have been appealed by the data's convenient availability and used it for quantitative research. However, as the inclusion of every single strength and concern dummy into econometric models would render the generation of hypotheses and the interpretation of results difficult, studies aggregate KLD dummy variables to be able to use it. Most of them simply add the number of 'strengths' and subtract the sum of 'concerns' to create a single CSR score (be it an overall index or one for single categories)[13]; others treat strengths and concerns as separate measures.[14]

Considering the structure of KLD data, at least three difficulties arise when the data are used as a proxy for CSP.[15] First, the weighting of single issues is controversial. When simply adding and/or subtracting strengths and concerns, all dimensions (issue-areas) are treated as equally important. Taking social performance as an example, this means that having a women or a member of a minority group as

[8] For their assessment, see Sect. 2.2.3.4.

[9] E.g. Berman et al. (1999).

[10] For a description of KLD's research methodology, see KLD Research (2007).

[11] As reported by Graves and Waddock (1994) and Hillman and Keim (2001), KLD formerly measured each issue-area on a five-points-scale ranging from 'major strength' (+2) to 'major weakness' (−2).

[12] These are *abortion, adult entertainment, alcohol, contraceptives, firearms, gambling, military, nuclear power* and *tobacco*.

[13] See for instance Chatterji et al. (2007); Graves and Waddock (1994); Hillman and Keim (2001); Waddock and Graves (1997).

[14] One problem here is that issue areas consist of different numbers of single items (dummies), which renders simple aggregate scores incomparable. Therefore, Mattingly and Berman (2006), normalise the scores by z-transforming each data point.

[15] For a harsh (and polemic) critique of KLD data's reliability, consistency and objectivity, see Entine (2003). See also the reply from Waddock (2003).

	strengths	concerns
Environmental Ratings		
Climate Change	no/yes (0/1)	no/yes (0/1)
Products and Services	no/yes (0/1)	no/yes (0/1)
Operations and Management	no/yes (0/1)	no/yes (0/1)
Other	no/yes (0/1)	no/yes (0/1)
Social Ratings		
Community	no/yes (0/1)	no/yes (0/1)
Diversity	no/yes (0/1)	no/yes (0/1)
Employee Relations	no/yes (0/1)	no/yes (0/1)
Human Rights	no/yes (0/1)	no/yes (0/1)
Product	no/yes (0/1)	no/yes (0/1)
Governance Ratings		
Reporting	no/yes (0/1)	no/yes (0/1)
Structure	no/yes (0/1)	no/yes (0/1)
Other	no/yes (0/1)	no/yes (0/1)
Controversial Business Involvement		
Involvement in nine controversial areas	involvement: no/yes (0/1)	

Fig. 3.3 KLD's corporate social responsibility rating scheme

CEO adds as much to a company's rating as undertaking 'outstanding or innovative initiatives primarily related to labor rights in its supply chain'.[16] To overcome these limitations, Ruf et al. (1998) developed a weighting scheme that has repeatedly been used since then.[17] It does, however, only attribute weights to the issue-areas, not to the single strengths and concerns within a given area. To remain in the example of human rights, this procedure still leads to an equal importance of the protection of minimum labour rights throughout the whole supply chain, on the one hand, and good relations to indigenous peoples at the other. An additional problem lies within the fact that there are no industry-specific weighting schemes: a number of environmental 'strengths' for a car-producer such as *Daimler Chrysler* count as much as the same number of 'strengths' at *Deutsche Bank*.

Second, the problem of weighting notwithstanding the practice of subtracting concerns from strengths presupposes that these variables measure the same constructs, that is they negatively co-vary. However, as Mattingly and Berman (2006) show, strengths and concerns often do not correlate and sometimes even co-vary positively. This can be seen as a strong indicator that these strengths and weaknesses are not two sides of the same underlying construct. A third limitation within

[16] KLD Research (2007), p. 8.

[17] Graves and Waddock (1994); Ruf et al. (2001); Waddock and Graves (1997).

KLD data can be seen in the use of dummy variables for the assessment of certain issues, which does not allow for detailed differentiation between inferior and superior performers within a single area. Given the problems described earlier, the popularity of KLD data in empirical research can probably as much be explained by their convenient availability as by their adequateness.

3.1.1.3 Adequateness of *oekom* Data and the Study of Glaser et al. (2007)

As with KLD data, *oekom*'s ratings were not specifically designed for the purpose of scientific studies. In principal, the same problems can therefore arise when used as secondary data for empirical analyses. However, concerning the three limitations identified with respect to KLD data, *oekom* data are arguably more suitable for such analyses due to differences in its specific structure.

First, when aggregating the single items from the lowest level to the over-all corporate responsibility grade on the first level of the rating (cf. Fig. 3.1), *oekom* uses industry-specific weighting schemes, which warrant that the single items and categories influence the rating according to their importance with respect to a given industry. For instance, monitoring suppliers for their environmental record is very important for the metals and mining industry but irrelevant to banks and financial institutions. *oekom*'s industry experts meet before each rating and discuss whether new or old weighting schemes adequately reflect current industry differences.[18] Second, *oekom* does not assess companies based on the absence or presence of certain strengths and weaknesses. It rather subdivides CSP dimensions into various categories over up to seven levels, and then grades companies concerning single items on the lowest level. Eventually, it uses these single item grades to construct dimensions finally resulting in the responsibility rating. Therefore, contrary to KLD data, scores do not have to be constructed by the researcher but are included in the data on each aggregation level. For instance, the analysis of CSP drivers in Sect. 3.2 will use the first and the second level of aggregation in the rating (*crr, scr, er*). One problem is, however, that the scores are not comparable across industries and therefore cannot be used for comparative statistics without being adjusted. This problem will be examined in Sect. 3.1.1.4. Third, the *oekom* rating system enables researchers to differentiate firm social performance *within single item scores*. The ratings take place on a 13-steps scale and are only weighted afterwards. Compared to dummy variables (absence/presence of strengths/concerns), this allows for differentiated comparisons concerning various companies' performance with regards to single items, categories and dimensions.[19]

[18] It is important to note that the use of industry-specific weighting schemes does *not* mean that the resulting scores would be comparable *across* industries. *oekom research*'s data is not suitable for evaluations such as 'BMW is better than Microsoft'.

[19] Such a differentiation is for instance needed when testing the hypothesis of decreasing marginal effects of CSP, cf. Sect. 3.5.

Although it is very common to use data from professional rating agencies such as KLD[20] and ARESE[21] for scientific studies on the CSP/CFP-link, and in spite of the adequateness of *oekom research* data for assessing CSP, only one published scientific study has so far been conducted based on these data. In one of their four independently conducted studies on the relationship between 'socially responsible or sustainable treatment of human resources'[22] and financial success, Glaser et al. (2007) use *oekom* data for their analysis. The study of Glaser et al. (2007) differs from this paper's approach with respect to various methodological aspects as will shortly be examined in the following.[23]

After testing the data's validity and reliability,[24] the authors proceed in four steps. First, they test for differences in financial performance (measured by ROI and EPS) between *oekom*'s best-in-class firms ('prime' status) and all other firms by means of a Mann–Whitney U-Test (however, without deriving hypotheses prior to the test). It is worth mentioning that this prime status is determined by the over-all corporate responsibility rating (CRR) grade, including environmental performance. Therefore, it is unclear how this relates to the research question, which explicitly focuses on human resources. In a second step, Spearman's rank correlation coefficients are computed for the association of financial measures, on the one side, and the overall CRR grade as well as three social sub-categories on the other.[25] No comprehensive model (e.g. regression analysis) is employed, which would be able to control for variables typically influencing performance measures. The problem with using *oekom*'s grades as absolute measures (rather than relative ones such as the best-in-class status) is that it compares grades across industries. As an example, this procedure considers an environmental score of 2.3 for a car producer to be 'better' than a score of 2.2 for an insurance.[26] Such a procedure runs counter

---

[20] For exemplary studies using KLD data for measuring CSP, cf. Barnett and Salomon (2006); Berman et al. (1999); Graves and Waddock (1994); Graves and Waddock (2000); Guerard (1997); Hillman and Keim (2001); Johnson and Greening (1999); Kurtz and DiBartolomeo (1996); Ruf et al. (2001); Turban and Greening (1997); Waddock and Graves (1997).

[21] Cf. Igalens and Gond (2005).

[22] Glaser et al. (2007), p. 47 (my translation).

[23] Apart from these differences, their data is derived from older *oekom research* ratings conducted from 2001 through 2003. So although the source of data is the same, we do not use the same sample.

[24] To test the data's validity, the authors employ a confirmatory factor analysis (CFA) and conclude that the two underlying constructs (social and environmental rating) are distinct factors and are well founded by the single indicators. However, such methods can be used only in the case of *reflective* indicators. But, considering *oekom*'s research method, these indicators are clearly *formative*. The *Frankfurt-Hohenheimer-Guidelines* research team aimed at developing an exhaustive set of various criteria that fully assesses a company's social and environmental performance. That is, the single dimensions are aggregated out of a complete set of single items that formatively construct these dimensions. The use of covariance based methods such as CFA in that context corresponds to a wrong specification and leads to inconsistent results. For a detailed discussion, cf. Albers and Hildebrandt (2006), Diamantopoulos and Winklhofer (2001) and Hermann et al. (2006).

[25] It remains unclear why the authors separate these categories after having argued that they coherently represent *one* construct (cronbach's α greater than 0.7).

[26] Concerning such comparisons across industries, see the discussion in Sect. 3.1.1.4.

to *oekom*'s best-in-class approach, which explicitly avoids direct between-industry grade comparisons.

Only in their third and fourth steps, Glaser et al. (2007) run separate correlation analyses for selected employees-related items and a sub-set of industries. That way, *ceteris paribus* effects (partial correlation coefficients) still cannot be analysed and the interpretation of the simple correlation coefficients is of very limited validity.[27]

3.1.1.4 Descriptive Statistics and Bivariate Analysis

According to *oekom research*'s business model, the relevant population consists of publicly traded companies. The original sample included 300 corporations from 13 industries and 24 different countries.[28] These companies were evaluated by *oekom research* in the years 2005 and 2006. Since these ratings are repeated only every third to fourth year, the results can be assumed to remain constant over 1 or 2 years. Time differences in the completion dates of single industry reports can therefore be neglected. Six companies had to be omitted due to restricted financial data availability. Table 3.1 provides an overview of the remaining sample's distribution with respect to industries and countries.

In line with the earlier argumentation,[29] *oekom* data were grouped according to stakeholders and used to construct respective components. To do this, numerical grades from the third level as depicted in Fig. 3.1 were weighted according to their relative importance in the *oekom* industry weighting schemes. The five stakeholder-related variables described later will be used throughout the empirical analyses in the next chapters.

The dimension *Staff and Suppliers* (variable: *staff*)[30] includes all social aspects regarding employees of the firm itself and those of its suppliers. The criteria according to which companies are rated include freedom of association, safeguarding jobs, payment, health and safety, equal opportunities, work-life balance, training and education, forced and child labour and measures taken by the firm to ensure similar standards at suppliers. *Society and Community* (*soc*) refers to the company's external relations with those communities that they are operating in. That concerns issues such as charitable contributions, political donations, stakeholder dialogue or human rights issues in the community not regarding the production process itself. *Corporate Governance and Business Ethics* (*corpgov*) comprises shareholder-related

---

[27] For problems with the interpretation of such coefficients of zero order, cf. Gujarati (2003), pp. 229–232.

[28] Compared to the total coverage of more than 800 companies that *oekom* rates, the 300 firms represent a limited sample. This is due to differences in the rating procedure: only a part of the firms is rated in a comprehensive way – the so-called inside-ratings – that allows for the differentiated analyses of this study. The other companies are evaluated in the 'outside-rating', which is based on a shorter and less in-depth analysis.

[29] Cf. Sects. 2.1.4 and 2.3.1.

[30] Throughout this section, variable names will be given in parentheses behind the full description. For an overview of all variables in use, cf. the appendix.

Table 3.1 Sample distribution with regards to countries and industries

	Automobile	Banking and financials	Chemicals	Food and beverages	Household products	Insurance	IT	Machinery	Metals and mining	Oil and gas	Pharma and biotech	Tele-communications	Transport and logistics	**Total**
AUS	–	3	–	–	–	2	–	–	1	1	–	1	–	**8**
AUT	–	2	–	–	–	–	–	–	1	1	–	1	–	**5**
BEL	–	2	1	1	–	–	–	–	–	–	–	–	–	**4**
BRA	–	1	–	–	–	–	–	–	–	–	–	–	–	**1**
CAN	–	4	–	–	–	–	–	–	2	5	–	2	–	**13**
CHE	–	3	1	1	–	4	–	2	–	–	3	1	–	**15**
DEU	5	5	4	–	2	2	2	1	2	–	3	1	2	**29**
DNK	–	1	–	2	–	–	–	–	–	–	2	1	–	**6**
ESP	–	2	–	–	–	1	–	–	–	1	–	1	1	**6**
FIN	–	–	–	–	–	1	–	1	1	–	–	–	–	**3**
FRA	2	2	1	3	1	2	1	–	–	1	1	1	1	**16**
GBR	–	10	1	5	1	5	–	–	5	3	2	3	3	**28**
HKG	–	–	–	–	–	–	–	–	–	–	–	–	1	**1**
IRL	–	2	–	–	–	1	–	–	–	–	–	–	–	**3**
ITA	1	2	–	–	–	1	–	–	–	1	–	1	–	**6**
JPN	6	4	3	2	2	3	7	5	3	–	1	1	2	**39**
KOR	1	–	–	–	–	–	–	–	1	–	–	–	–	**2**
NLD	–	2	2	1	–	1	1	–	1	–	1	1	1	**11**
NOR	–	–	1	–	–	1	–	–	–	2	–	1	–	**5**
PRT	–	–	–	–	–	–	–	–	–	–	–	1	–	**1**
SWE	–	4	–	–	–	–	–	3	–	–	–	1	–	**8**
TWN	–	–	–	–	–	–	1	–	–	–	–	–	–	**1**
USA	2	10	7	5	4	2	17	4	2	4	13	–	1	**61**
ZAF	–	2	–	–	–	–	–	–	–	–	–	–	–	**2**
Total	**17**	**41**	**21**	**20**	**10**	**26**	**29**	**16**	**19**	**19**	**26**	**18**	**12**	**$\sum = 294$**

aspects such as the independence of the board, shareholder democracy and the transparency of compensation schemes. It also refers to moral aspects of management, for example the existence and quality of codes of conducts, measures to ensure fair business conduct or major controversies (corruption, price fixing, antitrust). All social and environmental customer-related topics are included in the dimension *Social and Environmental Customer and Product Responsibility* (*cust*). This refers to aspects such as customer service (transparency and information), responsible marketing, the involvement of genetically modified food, the use of human stem cells, product safety and the environmental 'quality' of both the production process as well as the materials in use. *Environmental Management and Eco-efficiency* (*enman*) refers to the general quality of the company's environmental management, including its environmental policy, management systems, the monitoring of suppliers and reporting to external stakeholders. Furthermore, it includes eco-efficiency, which concerns the reduction of energy consumption, polluting emissions, etc.

Table 3.2 provides an overview of the distribution of grades along the single dimensions within each industry.

The original values of these dimensions (ranging from 1.0 to 4.0), however, cannot directly be used for the analyses without further transformation because of two reasons. First, as described earlier, these dimensions are not measured directly but are aggregated scores composed of up to 130 single items that are rated on a 13 points scale. Therefore, in spite of its seemingly metric scaling, the scale is inherently ordinal and distances between any grades are not equal. As ordinary-least-squares (OLS) regression presupposes a linear relation between the dependent and the independent variables and implies constant partial effects of the regressors, the variables cannot be used in their original scaling. Second, the original scores do not control for industry differences in the importance of the single dimensions. According to its best-in-class approach, *oekom research* does not directly compare grades of firms from different industries but only amongst companies within the same industry. Comparisons over industries are possible only after the translation of the grades into prime-status, which are not available at the level of data aggregation that is used in this study. Therefore, original scores were transformed into dummy variables taking value one if a given firm performs above the industry mean along single dimensions, and zero otherwise. This way, the dummies indicate low/high performance *per industry*, and can be included into OLS regression analyses.

Since the data allow for breaking down the overall company grade into single dimensions of CSR performance, it is interesting to ask whether companies typically perform well (low) on all dimensions or whether good (low) performance on one dimension does not necessarily come along with good (low) performance on the others. To analyse such interdependencies, simple correlation analyses were conducted. Table 3.3 reports Spearman's rank correlation coefficients, which measure the dependence of ordinal variables. It also displays *Cramer's V* for the transformed dichotomous variables.[31]

[31] Spearman's rank correlation analysis tests the dependency of variables in ordinal scales. Cramer's V measures the correlation between categorical variables such as binary variables

Table 3.2 Summary statistics for scores in each industry

	staff				*corpgov*				*soc*				*cust*				*enman*			
	min.	max.	s.d.	**mean**	min.	max.	s.d.	**mean**	min.	max.	s.d.	**mean**	min.	max.	s.d.	**mean**	min.	max.	s.d.	**mean**
Automobile	1.14	3.40	0.65	**2.18**	1.18	3.26	0.61	**2.17**	1.29	2.86	0.43	**2.12**	1.20	2.71	0.34	**1.90**	1.84	3.48	0.52	**2.65**
Banking and financials	1.26	3.07	0.47	**2.13**	1.63	3.61	0.51	**2.70**	1.13	3.63	0.53	**2.32**	1.00	2.57	0.34	**1.65**	1.00	3.43	0.58	**1.80**
Chemicals	1.21	2.97	0.50	**2.16**	1.52	3.69	0.67	**2.29**	1.00	3.29	0.56	**2.04**	1.00	3.04	0.50	**2.04**	1.11	3.51	0.60	**2.16**
Food and beverages	1.47	2.67	0.35	**2.04**	1.65	3.79	0.58	**2.69**	1.50	3.12	0.43	**2.28**	1.52	2.32	0.27	**1.88**	1.63	3.27	0.49	**2.35**
Household products	1.70	2.79	0.38	**2.19**	1.84	3.67	0.69	**2.84**	1.71	3.14	0.40	**2.53**	1.76	2.59	0.29	**2.10**	1.66	3.26	0.54	**2.47**
Insurance	1.56	3.15	0.38	**2.18**	1.54	3.13	0.45	**2.37**	1.38	2.88	0.39	**2.18**	1.21	2.84	0.42	**1.72**	1.21	3.20	0.45	**2.06**
IT	1.02	2.84	0.58	**1.65**	1.40	3.63	0.64	**2.71**	1.00	3.42	0.58	**2.03**	1.00	2.90	0.46	**1.71**	1.04	3.46	0.70	**1.92**
Machinery	1.07	2.69	0.43	**1.82**	1.78	3.67	0.54	**2.56**	1.38	2.78	0.40	**1.98**	1.51	3.04	0.43	**2.12**	1.47	3.36	0.56	**2.27**
Metals and mining	1.26	3.66	0.49	**2.36**	1.29	3.57	0.82	**2.56**	1.25	3.59	0.63	**2.12**	1.60	3.04	0.38	**2.17**	1.75	3.45	0.46	**2.57**
Oil and gas	1.77	3.30	0.44	**2.49**	1.65	3.86	0.78	**2.70**	1.68	3.62	0.55	**2.49**	1.37	2.54	0.35	**1.79**	1.49	3.19	0.52	**2.32**
Pharma and biotech	1.08	2.93	0.48	**2.12**	1.44	3.82	0.63	**2.19**	1.00	2.79	0.46	**1.84**	1.00	2.31	0.38	**1.51**	1.04	3.65	0.85	**2.16**
Tele-communi cations	1.75	3.65	0.52	**2.54**	1.54	3.67	0.55	**2.37**	1.08	3.13	0.55	**2.41**	1.33	2.88	0.41	**2.09**	1.74	3.50	0.44	**2.32**
Transport and logistics	1.57	2.58	0.29	**2.24**	1.32	3.56	0.66	**2.28**	1.79	2.50	0.26	**2.12**	1.34	2.40	0.31	**1.82**	1.58	2.56	0.28	**1.98**

Table 3.3 Tests for statistical dependency between CSP-variables

	scr	*staff*	*corpgov*	*soc*	*cust*	*enman*
Correlation of single CSP dimensions (dummies)[a]						
er	**0.5041**					
	(0.000)					
corpgov		0.0256	1.0000			
		(0.660)				
soc		**0.4100**	0.0523	1.0000		
		(0.000)	(0.370)			
cust		**0.3873**	−0.0871	**0.3446**	1.0000	
		(0.000)	(0.135)	(0.000)		
enman		**0.4215**	−0.091	**0.5126**	**0.4756**	1.0000
		(0.000)	(0.119)	(0.000)	(0.000)	
Correlation of single CSP dimensions (orig. scale)[b]						
er	**0.4990**					
	(0.000)					
corpgov		0.0532	1.0000			
		(0.363)				
soc		**0.5103**	**0.2173**	1.0000		
		(0.000)	(0.000)			
cust		**0.4269**	−0.0326	**0.3840**	1.0000	
		(0.000)	(0.578)	(0.000)		
enman		**0.3921**	−0.014	**0.4423**	**0.4123**	1.0000
		(0.000)	(0.811)	(0.000)	(0.000)	

[a] Values report Cramer's V. *p*-values of Pearson's Chi-Squared-Test are given in parentheses. Bold figures are significantly dependent on the 1% level. *crr*, *scr* and *err* correspond to the original *oekom* ratings on the first and second level (cf. Fig. 3.1) and will be used for the analysis in Sect. 3.2 (correlations to the other variables are therefore not relevant). *staff*, *corpgov*, *soc*, *cust* and *enman* are the stakeholder-related variables, which will be used in all other analyses

[b] Values report Spearman's rank correlation coefficient. *p*-values are given in parentheses. Bold numbers are significantly dependet on the 1% level

In addition to the five single components discussed up to here, Table 3.3 also reports correlations between the two main sub-dimensions of the over-all rating, which are used in the analysis of potential drivers of CSP in Sect. 3.2. The two dimensions out of which the *oekom Corporate Responsibility Rating* (*crr*) is constructed, are the *Social Cultural Rating* (*scr*), on the one hand, and the *Environmental Rating*(*er*), on the other.[32]

Although variance is lost through the procedure of dichotomising the original variables, results hardly vary from continuous to binary scaling. In both cases there is a significant dependency between performance in the social cultural rating and the environmental rating. Concerning the five stakeholder-related components, all

(as is the case here). The respective χ^2-test analyses the null hypothesis that the variables are independent. Cf. Backhaus et al. (2006), pp. 242 et sqq.

[32] Since higher aggregated scores are entirely constructed out of the lower-level grades, it would not make sense to compute correlations between different levels. The respective fields in Table 3.3 are therefore left blank. For a clarification of the relation between the grades, recall Fig. 3.1 on p. 35.

variables but *Corporate Governance and Business Ethics* (*corpgov*) significantly correlate with each other, indicating that companies typically perform well (low) on more than one CSR component. This result suggests the conclusion that management generally follows coherent CSR strategies, because there are probably synergies to gain when performing well on multiple CSP components.

One explanation for the exception of *corpgov* could be that shareholder management traditionally belongs to good management independent of CSR, that is management might consider good corporate governance as important without subscribing to the notion of CSR in general.

3.1.2 Financial Performance: Tobin's Q

As examined in Sect. 2.2.3, various accounting- and market-based measures have been used in earlier work to proxy corporate financial performance. In the context of this study, it is most appropriate to use a market-based measure for corporate success: if CSP proves to have any effect on financial performance, it should best be measured by considering the market's assessment of a company's value, which includes all relevant expectations with that regard. To see whether results change when an accounting number is used instead of market values, return on equity (ROE) will be used for various robustness checks throughout the analysis.

A frequently applied market-based measure for firm performance is *Tobin's Q*, which is defined as the ratio of the market value of assets to their replacement value at the end of the most recent fiscal year.[33] There has been a long debate on how to adequately compute *Tobin's Q*. Lindenberg and Ross (1981) suggested a precise formula which, however, requires difficult to obtain data to measure the replacement value. Chung and Pruitt (1994) developed a proxy that is much easier to obtain and still yields very similar results. In line with the latter approach and following previous studies, the market value of assets is proxied by the book values of assets (*TA*) minus the book value of equity (*CE*) minus deferred taxes (*DefTax*) plus the market value of common stocks (*MV*). The replacement value of assets is proxied by the book value of assets (*TA*)[34]:

$$Tobin's\ Q = \frac{TA - CE - DefTax + MV}{TA}$$

Market values are year end values, book values were taken from the most recent annual report of the same year but not later than September 30. Thereby, it is

[33] For empirical studies using *Tobin's Q*, see, for example Black et al. (2006); Bauer et al. (2004); Claessens et al. (2002); Gompers et al. (2003); Gorton and Schmid (2000); La Porta et al. (2002); Lang and Litzenberger (1989); McConnell and Servaes (1990); Morck et al. (1988). Although *Tobin's Q* is a standard measure in the finance literature, it has rarely been used in the CSR context. For exceptions, see Dowell et al. (2000), Hillman and Keim (2001) and Luo and Bhattacharya (2006).

[34] Gompers et al. (2003), p. 151; Kaplan and Zingales (1997); La Porta et al. (2002), p. 1156.

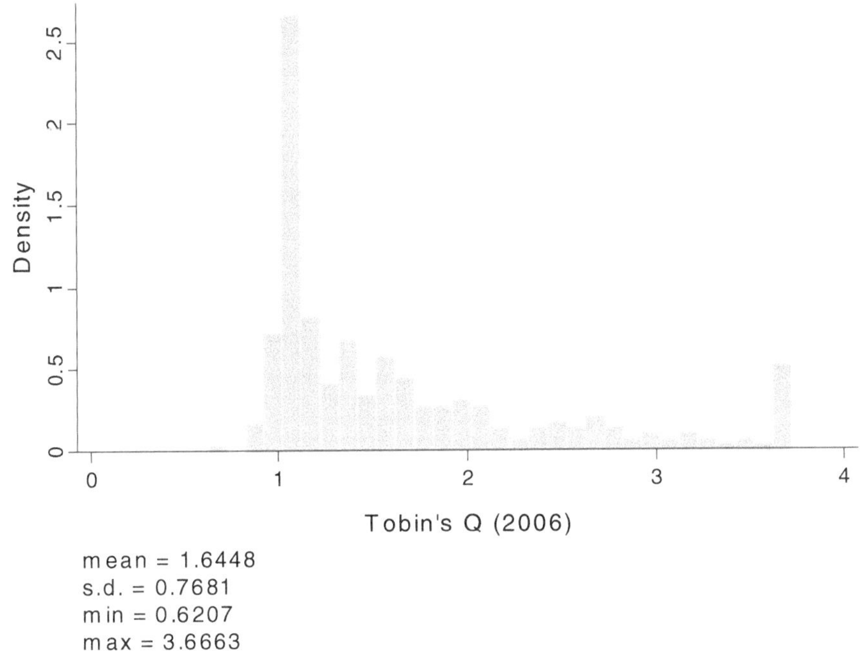

Fig. 3.4 Histogram for the distribution of *Tobin's Q* in 2006

warranted that the market was able to proceed and evaluate the published data. To avoid large outliers, *Tobin's Q* was censored at the 95th percentile.[35] All financial data were obtained from the databases *Thomson Worldscope* and *Datastream*. The histogram displayed in Fig. 3.4 shows the right-skewed distribution of *Tobin's Q* (2006) in the sample with descriptive statistics.

3.1.3 Control Variables and Return on Equity

As will be discussed in more detail later, variance in the dependent variable *Tobin's Q* has to be explained by taking into account several factors. Market risk, firm size and leverage are known to have an influence on market-based performance measures and were therefore included in the OLS regression models as control variables.[36]

A company's market risk (variable: *risk*) was measured as the firm's stock dependence on market performance. In line with the Capital Asset Pricing Model (CAPM), Betas for 2006 were calculated by regressing company stock returns on

[35] See McConnell and Servaes (1990), p. 600 or La Porta et al. (2002), p. 1158.

[36] Cf. Sect. 3.3.2.1. and the literature cited there.

market returns on a daily basis:[37]

$$\left(\frac{RI_t - RI_{t-1}}{RI_{t-1}} - i_{RF,t}\right) = \beta_0 + \beta_1 \left(\frac{BI_t - BI_{t-1}}{BI_{t-1}} - i_{RF,t}\right), \text{ where}$$

$RI_t =$ Return index for a given company at day t.
$i_{RF,t} =$ Risk-free interest rate at day t (1-month-Libor for respective currency; government bond, if Libor not available).
$BI_t =$ Benchmark index at day t (market index in respective country).

Firm size (*size*) was measured by sales in million US$ to warrant comparability, and leverage (*lev*) was computed as the ratio of total debt to total assets.[38] Although *Tobin's Q* will be used as a measure of firm financial performance throughout the analysis, return on equity (*roe*) as an accounting measure will be used as an explanatory variable in Sect. 3.2 and for robustness checks of the OLS regression results in later chapters. Table 3.4 provides descriptive statistics for the three control variables and *roe* (2005 and 2006).[39]

For the sake of interpretability of the constant and the slope coefficients in the OLS regression analysis, the control variables were mean-centred, resulting in the distribution summarised in Table 3.5.

Table 3.4 Summary statistics for original control variables and *roe*

Distribution of control variables (original values) and roe				
Variable	Mean	Std. dev.	Min	Max
risk	1.051	0.418	0.037	2.318
size (log)	9.592	1.218	5.941	12.701
lev	0.659	0.239	0.116	1.104
roe_{2005}	15.868	8.584	0.367	34.179
roe_{2006}	17.216	8.416	2.166	33.750

Table 3.5 Summary statistics for control variables after transformation

Distribution of control variables (mean-centered)				
Variable	Mean	Std. dev.	Min	Max
risk	0.000	0.418	−1.013	1.268
size (log)	0.000	1.218	−3.651	3.110
lev	0.000	0.239	−0.543	0.446

[37] Concerning the foundations of the CAPM, see Sharpe (1964); Lintner (1965); Mossin (1966).

[38] To warrant constant partial effects of *size* on the dependent variable in the OLS analysis, log values of sales were used, cf. Sect. 3.3.3.1.

[39] *roe* values were censored at the 1 and 99% quantiles to avoid large outlayers.

3.2 Determinants of Corporate Social Performance

3.2.1 Model Specification and Hypotheses

Before analysing the effects of superior CSP, it is worthwhile asking what factors actually determine whether a given company performs high on a CSP dimension, that is what the drivers of CSP are. As argued earlier, it is for instance conceivable that larger firms have higher incentives to invest in their social performance and that CSP varies between industries and with the companies' different legal and/or cultural backgrounds.[40] These CSP drivers, the influence of which will be analysed in the following chapter, generally fall into two broad categories that either concern a company's *ability* or its *necessity* to address CSR issues.

The *first category* mainly refers to a company's financial performance. CSR is sometimes seen as a discretionary management task, which a company can only afford if it is financially successful.[41] In this view, past financial performance is a necessary condition for the company's ability to display a high CSP and should therefore partly predict the belonging to the high or low performing group. A number of empirical studies has analysed the partial effect of financial performance as an antecedent of CSP, measuring financial performance by accounting numbers such as return on assets (ROA), sales (ROS) or equity (ROE). Most of these studies indeed find a positive relation.[42] Others, however, only find a relation to certain CSP components or entirely fail to support any such relation.[43] To measure firm financial performance, the analyses in the next chapter use an accounting number rather than a market measure, because ROE is a measure of profitability and therefore determines how many resources are available to be spent during the next period.

In addition to past financial performance, some authors suggest that the company's ownership structure has an influence on CSP.[44] Therefore, the debt-to-equity ratio (*lev*) is included in the analysis to control for differences in the capital structure and their influence on CSP. Past CSP is another factor that influences the company's current ability to receive high scores at the *oekom* ratings. Since it requires substantial know-how and financial resources to build competencies that allow for a good CSP,[45] past performance should explain a significant part of current social and environmental performance. As past CSR grades are available for a subset of 128 companies within the original sample, it can be included in the analysis of this sub-sample as an explanatory variable.

---

[40] See, for instance, Alberini and Segerson (2002) or Waddock and Graves (1997).

[41] For a thorough discussion of this 'slack resources' argument, see Sects. "Tracing Causality: The Direction of the CSP/CFP-Link" and 3.3.3.3.

[42] Deckop and Merriman (2006); Orlitzky et al. (2003); Waddock and Graves (1997).

[43] Johnson and Greening (1999) only find a relation to a people-related (as opposed to a product-related) CSP component. McGuire et al. (1988, 2003) show no clear relation.

[44] Cf. Atkinson and Galaskiewicz (1988), Graves and Waddock (1994), and Johnson and Greening (1999).

[45] Cf. McWilliams and Siegel (2001), pp. 123–124.

A *second category* of CSP drivers concerns the company's need, rather than its ability, to foster its relations to various stakeholders. Firm visibility for instance can be expected to determine a company's likelihood to be targeted by the media and pressure groups lobbying for labour rights or environmental protection. In 2003, sportswear-producer *Puma* was pressed by a non-governmental organisation (NGO) to help one of its Mexican supplying manufacturers prevent bankruptcy and ensure the payment of the workers' full wages, although it only accounted for a minor fraction of this supplier's sales. The remaining orders were from a U.S./Mexican textile company that had itself gone bankrupt and apparently was not suitable for NGO campaigns due to its being little-known.[46] This example illustrates how brand vulnerability of large firms can increase a company's need to be prepared to handle moral conflicts, that is to socially perform well. In the following, firm visibility is proxied by a company's size (measured by sales), which has repeatedly been included as a control variable in previous empirical studies.[47] However, only a few of these studies revealed significant relations between firm size and CSP.[48]

Another factor that might determine a company's necessity to invest into its CSP is its market risk. Orlitzky and Benjamin (2001) for instance assume that CSP works as an insurance and thus lowers risks. Additionally, they also argue that lower risk leads to higher CSP because reduced risk leaves more resources to be spent for CSR. In contrast to some previous primary studies, their meta-study finds a negative relation with CSP in general.[49] Finally, the firm's cultural and legal background can be assumed to have an influence on the company's CSP level. National and international regulations such as the Sarbanes-Oxley-Act or European legal requirements include social and environmental issues that could explain regional differences in CSP levels.[50] The region of the firm is therefore captured by two dummy variables: European companies are the reference group, *cont* takes value 1 if the firm is from the US or Australia and *cont2* takes value 1 if it comes from any other country.

To analyse the influence of the potential CSP drivers discussed earlier, the following chapter's analyses regress CSP variables on the variables discussed up to this point.[51] Waddock and Graves (1997) suggest to further include industry-specific

[46] The Clean Clothes Campaign provides detailed information on that case, see http://www.cleanclothes.org/appeals-archive.htm#Matamoros.

[47] Size has not only been included as a proxy for firm visibility. It also has been included based on the argument that larger firms have more resources available to build competencies related to CSR. The following analysis captures this notion by including past financial performance as a regressor.

[48] Deckop and Merriman (2006) and Waddock and Graves (1997) include size variables which do not show any significant relation. In contrast, Johnson and Greening (1999), McGuire et al. (1988) and McGuire et al. (2003) do find a positive relation.

[49] Their analysis also reveals that this negative relation with CSP is smaller if CSP is measured as environmental performance. For studies that do *not* find a significant relation between risk and CSP, cf. Alexander and Buchholz (1978) and Waddock and Graves (1997).

[50] Alberini and Segerson (2002); McWilliams and Siegel (2001), p. 122.

[51] Deckop and Merriman (2006) and McGuire et al. (2003) further include the CEO pay structure and their incentives schemes in their analysis of CSP drivers. For lack of such data for the sample employed here, this variable cannot be controlled for in the study.

determinants of CSP into the analysis. Since *oekom* data are based on a best-in-class approach, such data cannot be employed in this study, though.[52]

To warrant a differentiated analysis, three models are tested in the following, which use the performance on different CSP components based on the ratings of *oekom research*.[53] The first model uses the overall Corporate Responsibility Rating (*crr*) upon which *oekom research* gives its investment recommendations. Although it has been and further will be argued that it is not useful to include this CSP over-all grade as a *regressor* when explaining financial performance, it can be meaningfully used as the *dependent* variable. Because the point of interest here is whether there are systematic differences between those firms that are recommended by an SRI rating agency such as *oekom research*, and those that are not. To see whether results change when the environmental and social components of the over-all grade are separately analysed, two more models are computed using the social-cultural (*scr*) and the environmental rating (*er*) as dependent variables, respectively.[54]

Since these three CSP components are binary dependent variables, nonlinear regression functions are more suitable than using ordinary least squares (OLS) estimation. One such function is the probit regression, which estimates the probability that an observation takes value 1 in the binary dependent variable, conditional on the values of a set of explanatory variables.[55]

The three population probit models actually to be estimated then include multiple regressors as shown by the following equations:[56]

$$\Pr(crr = 1|x_1, x_2, \ldots, x_6, crr_{\text{lagged}}) = \Phi\left(\beta_0 + \sum_{i=1}^{6} \beta_i x_i + \beta_7 crr_{\text{lagged}}\right) \quad (1)$$

$$\Pr(scr = 1|x_1, x_2, \ldots, x_6, scr_{\text{lagged}}) = \Phi\left(\beta_0 + \sum_{i=1}^{6} \beta_i x_i + \beta_7 scr_{\text{lagged}}\right) \quad (2)$$

$$\Pr(er = 1|x_1, x_2, \ldots, x_6, er_{\text{lagged}}) = \Phi\left(\beta_0 + \sum_{i=1}^{6} \beta_i x_i + \beta_7 er_{\text{lagged}}\right), \quad (3)$$

where Φ is the cumulative standard normal distribution function. *crr*, *scr* and *er* correspond to the *oekom* corporate responsibility, social cultural and environmental ratings, respectively, and

$$\begin{aligned} x_1 &= risk \\ x_2 &= size \\ x_3 &= lev \\ x_4 &= cont \\ x_5 &= cont2 \\ x_6 &= roe_{2005}. \end{aligned}$$

[52] Cf. Sect. 3.1.1.

[53] Concerning the construction of the two performance-classes, cf. 3.1.1.4.

[54] To see the location of these three components within the *oekom* rating, recall Fig. 3.1.

[55] Stock and Watson (2007), pp. 389–394.

[56] For a formal description of the case of multiple regressors, cf. Wooldridge (2002), pp. 457–458.

To better illustrate the logic behind probit regression, the following considers the case of only one regressor by asking how a company's belonging to the high performing class depends on its previous *oekom* grade. For better visualisation, the lagged values are kept in the original scale (metric, ranging from values 1 to 4), whereas the current rating is transformed into a binary variable (performance class). Formally, the probit population model is expressed by the following equation:

$$\Pr(crr = 1 | crr_{\text{lagged}}) = \Phi(\beta_0 + \beta_1 crr_{\text{lagged}}), \tag{4}$$

where, as before, Φ is the cumulative standard normal distribution function. The constant and the coefficient are estimated by the method of maximum likelihood, which produces consistent and efficient estimators. Using the estimated coefficients, the probability for $crr = 1$ can be computed for every observation, given its previous rating grade. The grey dotted line in Fig. 3.5 corresponds to these fitted values. The black dots indicate the actual values for past (continuous) and current (binary) *crr* performance in the sample. As the graph shows, receiving high grades during the last rating process increases the estimated probability of belonging to the high performance group.

After this illustration, the next sections will return to the estimation of (1)–(3), which represent the actual models of interest.

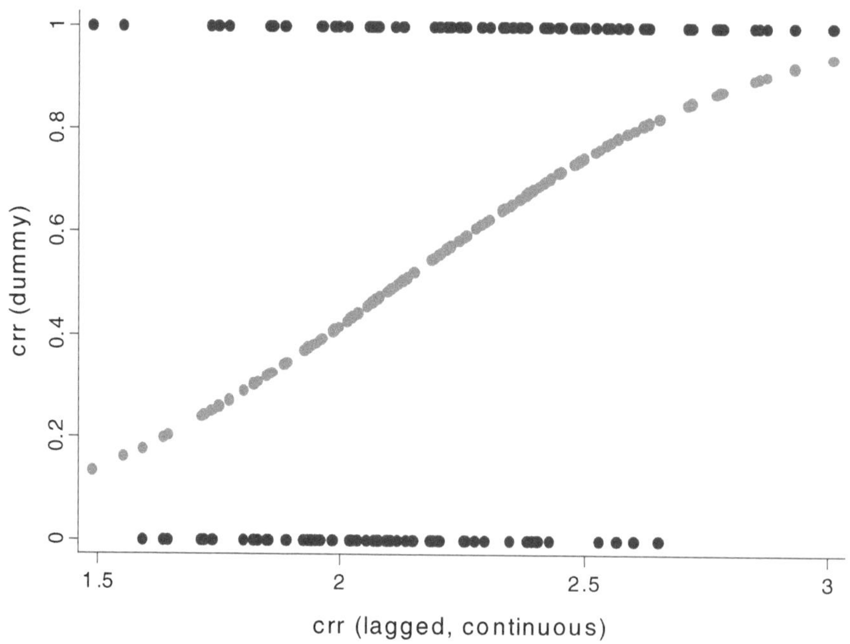

Fig. 3.5 Probit model of the probability of 'high rating', given past rating

3.2.2 Bivariate Analysis

Table 3.6 gives an overview of the relevant pair-wise correlations between the variables used in the probit regression models.[57]

As the correlation coefficients show, there is no significant dependency between *risk* and any of the CSP variables, neither actual nor past ones. *Size* and *lev* are both positively and significantly correlated with the actual ratings (with the exception of the relation between *lev* and *er*) but not with the past ones. As expected, there is a strong correlation between current and past performance with regards to both the over-all grade and the subcomponents. The weakest correlation between past and current performance exists within the social-cultural component; an issue that will also be discussed in the next chapter. To analyse whether these correlations still persist after controlling for other sample differences, the following chapter will analyse partial correlations to explore the dependencies between CSP and the variables discussed earlier.

Table 3.6 Pair-wise correlations

	Matrix of pair-wise correlation between variables used in the probit regression models								
	crr	crr_{lagged}	*scr*	scr_{lagged}	*er*	er_{lagged}	*risk*	*size*	*lev*
crr_{lagged}	**0.4040**	1.0000							
	0.0000								
scr_{lagged}			**0.1758**	1.0000					
			(0.0472)						
er_{lagged}					**0.4377**	1.0000			
					(0.0000)				
risk	−0.0357	−0.0660	0.0016	−0.0288	0.0002	0.0990	1.0000		
	(0.5419)	(0.4595)	(0.9783)	(0.7471)	(0.9969)	(0.2664)			
size	**0.2724**	0.0898	**0.1573**	−0.0123	**0.2392**	−0.0298	**−0.1768**	1.0000	
	(0.0000)	(0.3137)	(0.0069)	(0.8903)	(0.0000)	(0.7388)	(0.0023)		
lev	**0.1692**	0.0727	**0.1605**	0.0684	0.0700	−0.0520	**−0.1490**	**0.3669**	1.0000
	(0.0036)	(0.4149)	(0.0058)	(0.4428)	(0.2312)	(0.5602)	(0.0105)	(0.0000)	
cont	**−0.1431**	**−0.2053**	−0.0926	−0.0922	**−0.2074**	**−0.1936**			
	(0.0141)	(0.0201)	(0.1130)	(0.3008)	(0.0003)	(0.0286)			
cont2	**−0.1569**	**−0.2670**	**−0.2651**	**−0.2844**	−0.0761	−0.1393			
	(0.0070)	(0.0023)	(0.0000)	(0.0011)	(0.1931)	(0.1168)			
roe_{2005}	0.0470	0.0331	0.0496	0.0848	0.0268	−0.0003	**−0.1237**	**0.1300**	0.0338
	(0.4225)	(0.7105)	(0.3973)	(0.3411)	(0.6473)	(0.9973)	(0.0339)	(0.0258)	(0.5633)

Note: Values report Bravais–Pearson correlation coefficients for those variables that appear together in one model. Significance levels are given in parantheses. Bold numbers indicate that variables are significant on the 5% level or below

[57] Point-biserial correlation coefficients show the correlation between a binary and a continuous variable. The formula is mathematically equivalent to the Bravais–Pearson correlation formula if it uses the empirical standard deviation of the metric variable. Cf. Jann (2005), p. 91.

3.2.3 Probit Regression: Results and Discussion

In accordance with the discussion of the previous chapter, three probit regression functions are estimated by maximum-likelihood. The first model regresses the overall corporate responsibility rating (*crr*) on lagged *crr* values as well as on the set of variables reviewed earlier. Models 2 and 3 use the two sub-categories social-cultural rating (*scr*) and environmental rating (*er*) as the dependent variable, leaving the set of regressors unaltered with the exception of the lagged *scr* and *er* values. Table 3.7 reports the results of these regressions, where columns 1–3 correspond to the three respective models.

As expected after the last chapter's discussion, *size* and crr_{lagged} are strong drivers of the current *crr* rating, which becomes clear through their significantly

Table 3.7 Probit regression results

Dependant variable	*crr*	*scr*	*er*
Regressors			
risk	−0.0777	0.1406	0.0990
	(0.8080)	(0.6490)	(0.7700)
size	0.2618**	0.0679	0.3182***
	(0.0140)	(0.4910)	(0.0030)
lev	0.3820	0.8680	−0.1328
	(0.5430)	(0.1450)	(0.8320)
cont	−0.1854	−0.0627	−0.5505*
	(0.5580)	(0.8220)	(0.0970)
cont2	−0.2063	−0.6895*	−0.6409
	(0.6110)	(0.0920)	(0.1160)
roe_{2005}	0.0043	0.0065	0.0063
	(0.7680)	(0.6310)	(0.6850)
crr_{lagged}	0.9972***		
	(0.0000)		
scr_{lagged}		0.3114	
		(0.1970)	
er_{lagged}			1.1589***
			(0.0000)
constant	−0.5125	−0.0706	−0.5745*
	(0.1220)	(0.8240)	(0.0900)
Δ Prob	0.3814	0.1216	0.4356
N	128	128	128
Wald (Prob > χ^2)	0.0001***	0.1613	0.0000***
LR (Prob > χ^2)	0.0001***	0.1287	0.0000***
correct [%]	0.6719	0.6172	0.7031
Pseudo-R^2	0.1733	0.0644	0.2253

The three probit regressions were estimated by maximum likelihood. *p*-values ($P > z$) are reported in parentheses (calculated with heteroscedasticity-robust standard errors). Individual coefficients are statistically significant at the *10%, **5% or ***1% level (two-tailed *t*-test). Δ Prob gives the difference in predicted probability of $crr = 1$ ($scr = 1$, $er = 1$), low vs. high past performers, for an average European company. Correct [%] gives the percentage of correctly classified observations by the estimated function

positive coefficients in column 1. Equation (1) shows that these estimated regression coefficients are not as easily interpretable as in the case of OLS. To illustrate the effect of high past ratings on current ratings, one can consider how the predicted probability of a high *oekom* rating (i.e. $crr = 1$) changes with the past rating for the case of a European company that has the sample average values of all the regressors other than past *crr* performance (cf. the row of Δ Prob in Table 3.7).[58] For instance, the predicted probability of $crr = 1$ for such an average company increases by 38% if one compares past low with past high performers.

In contrast to the results of Orlitzky and Benjamin (2001), but consistent with the findings of the previous bivariate analysis, *risk* does not significantly determine a company's over-all CSP. However, as opposed to the earlier correlation analysis, the probit regression reveals no significant relation between *lev* and *crr* after holding constant *size* and crr_{lagged}. The same applies to the regional background variables *cont* and *cont2*, which display no significant coefficient estimates. This does not necessarily imply that legal and cultural backgrounds do not influence CSP. Rather, the results indicate that these dummies do not reflect cultural and/or legal differences well enough to measure their precise influence on the CSP level. Unfortunately, because of the limited sample size and uneven distribution of nationalities (cf. Table 3.1), a more differentiated analysis of such national differences is not possible.

Surprisingly and in contradiction to the 'slack resources' argument as well as to some of the previous studies cited earlier, the coefficient of past financial performance, measured by return on equity, is not statistically significant. This result is robust to changes in the measure of financial performance, as including *Tobin's Q* from 2005 did not yield significant coefficients either. Given the widely assumed bi-directional causal relation between corporate social and financial performance, this is an interesting result.[59]

Concerning the significance of the model altogether, several procedures are available to test for the quality of the model (test statistics for the following procedures are reported in the last rows of Table 3.7). First, the Wald-test as well the likelihood-ratio tests both fail to reject the null hypothesis that the vector of estimated parameters equals zero so that it can be assumed to significantly add explanatory power to a model which only includes the intercept.[60] Furthermore, the Pseudo-R^2 of 17.30% is a reasonable though not very high value.[61] Another possibility to intuitively evaluate the goodness-of-fit of the estimated model to the sample

[58] Technically, the two predicted probabilities are compared by computing the respective values of the cumulative standard normal distribution function according to (1): once for $crr_{lagged} = 0$ and once for $crr_{lagged} = 1$.

[59] Concerning this bi-directional relation, cf. Sect. "Tracing Causality: The Direction of the CSP/CFP-Link" and 3.3.3.3.

[60] The Wald test and the likelihood ratio test are two asymptotically equivalent test procedures when maximum likelihood estimation is employed. Cf. Greene (2003), pp. 484–488.

[61] In contrast to R^2 in OLS, the Pseudo-R^2 cannot be interpreted as the fraction of explained variance. Rather, it compares two estimated likelihood functions: one where all the explanatory variables are included and one restricted function with only the intercept. It thereby indicates the explanatory power of the regressors. Cf. Gujarati (2003), pp. 605–607.

is to look at the quality of the predicted classification. Values in the row *correct [%]* in Table 3.7 indicate how many observations are correctly classified, if the classification predicted by the estimated function is compared to that of the sample.[62] Finally, the analysis is robust to changes in the assumed underlying distribution.[63]

As reported in columns (2) and (3), results change as soon as the analysis is shifted to a less aggregated level by decomposing the *crr* grade into its two sub-categories social-cultural (*scr*) and environmental rating (*er*). Apparently, although the over-all rating is well predicted by the previous rating, this relation is mainly due to the environmental rating component. Concerning the social component, the regressors fail to predict the classification in the *crr* performance groups. The Wald test and the likelihood ratio test as well as the low Pseudo-R^2 suggest that the model altogether is not valid as the joint hypothesis that the estimated parameters equal zero cannot be rejected on a reasonable significance level. In contrast, the third regression model taking *er* as the dependent binary variable shows very good quality measures and qualitatively identical results compared to the first column. One difference is the negative *cont* coefficient, which is significant at the 10% level and therefore suggests that European corporations are less likely to be rated high on the environmental performance ranking. Although it is not entirely clear that this result is not merely random, it is consistent with the fact that European countries typically have comparably strict environmental regulation.

The comparison of the two sub-component models suggests that the social-cultural rating is more likely to change over time than the environmental performance (which was already indicated by the lower correlation of *scr* and scr_{lagged} in the previous chapter). One reason for why it is easier to improve (or decline) on the social performance is that such changes presumably are not as costly and know-how-dependent as efforts to induce changes in environmental performance.

3.3 Empirical Evidence for a Differentiated CSP/CFP-Link

3.3.1 Hypotheses

Empirical dependence techniques cannot in itself generate scientific claims as to the relation between various phenomena. To test for empirical correlations, one first needs well-founded hypotheses that are grounded in substantial theories.[64] The following section derives hypotheses as to how variance in firm financial performance, here measured by *Tobin's Q*, might best be explained empirically. In the course of this, it first discusses the actual variables of interest, namely those

[62] Since the fitted values continuously range from 0 to 1, observations are classified according to the criterion: $\overline{\overline{crr}} = \begin{cases} 1, \text{if } \Pr(crr = 1) > 0.5 \\ 0, \text{if } \Pr(crr = 1) < 0.5 \end{cases}$, where $\overline{\overline{crr}}$ corresponds to the predicted classification.

[63] The regression was also performed with a logit function and yielded qualitatively identical results as the probit model. Results are not reported.

[64] Cf. Gujarati (2003), p. 74[14].

concerning corporate social performance, before it asks about the expected influence of control variables that are known to typically influence *Tobin's Q*. Finally, in line with the contingency approach mentioned earlier, it develops arguments concerning interaction effects.

3.3.1.1 Corporate Social Performance Variables

The Neoclassical Approach Vs. the Business Case Hypothesis

Within the long-lasting academic discussion on CSR, opinions on CSR and arguments on its relation to financial performance not only differed at any given point in time but also have changed throughout the course of the debate. After the normative notion of corporate social and environmental obligations to society had slowly reached the academic debate,[65] arguments against such an assumption quickly entered the stage and still continue to exist in more recent publications.[66] Many of these arguments are developed within the neoclassical paradigm of the profit-maximising firm, the only goal of which is to satisfy the shareholders' interests. According to this view, investments in social goals constitute an illegitimate expenditure of resources that lowers the shareholders' value. In line with this reasoning, superior CSP can only happen at the expense of corporate profits and should therefore be expected to come along with lower financial performance.[67]

An underlying assumption of these Friedman-style arguments is the divergence of the firm's private economic interests, on the one hand, and public social interests on the other. From that perspective, managers face the choice of two mutually exclusive decisions: *either* maximising profits *or* admitting and pursuing social responsibilities. This might have been an applicable assumption at a time when CSR was rather a new notion, the acceptance of which was not expected from influential stakeholders in society. Then, CSR expenditures could rightly be considered as the manager's private interest, which was not necessarily the reason he was hired for. As long as the persecution of social goals was not in the shareholder's private interest, these were a violation of the contract between the shareholder and the manager.

Nowadays, however, spending resources for CSR can in some cases perfectly fit the profit-maximising calculus of companies. As will be shown later, management's decision to invest in CSR can be in the company's very own interest for two reasons. It can on the one hand be argued that CSP triggers positive consequences, for example by enabling the company to access new markets. On the other hand, good CSP can help avoiding negative effects such as consumer boycotts or NGO campaigns. From that perspective, CSR is nothing else than risk management. These arguments,

[65] Cf. Bowen (1953); Chamberlain (1973); Davis (1960); Davis (1967); McGuire (1963); Walton (1967).

[66] See the literature cited in footnote 5 on p. 1.

[67] For arguments focussing on the costs of CSR, cf. McWilliams and Siegel (2001), p. 124.

basically assuming a convergence between doing *good* and doing *well*, have become known as the business case hypothesis.[68]

But even if one accepts the basic idea that improving CSP can be in the shareholder's interest, the question still remains whether the benefits from CSR investments outweigh their costs. Examples of arguments supporting the assumption of a positive CSP/CFP-link abound. Very few, however, have been developed within a coherent conceptual or theoretical framework. One example for such a framework is the application of the resource-based view to CSR matters.[69] It considers CSR as a resource or competence that allows the firm to gain competitive advantages by combining internal strengths and external opportunities. Another example is the aforementioned stakeholder approach that has often been used to justify the existence of a positive CSP/CFP-link.[70] Applied in a generic way, however, such approaches do not capture the single mechanisms that would help explain and understand a positive or a negative association between corporate social and financial performance. There is no obvious reason to assume that such a direct relation exists *per se*. Even the stakeholder approach needs to explain why good relations with stakeholders should improve financial performance. Why would a good relation to the community (as one important stakeholder) *in itself* have a positive financial impact for the firm? If such a link exists, it can only be explained with reference to indirect effects such as improved reputation, which in turn improves customer loyalty, or the ability to recruit and retain skilled and motivated employees in the community. As argued in Sect. 2.3.4, only such mediating mechanisms can explain the indirect relation between CSP and CFP.

As with the components of CSP, mediating effects can be described and distinguished with reference to Stakeholder Theory. This is not to say, however, that stakeholder orientation necessarily corresponds with the 'mechanisms'. Employee satisfaction will not only be influenced by a good staff orientation, but also by the company's amount of charitable giving, its legal integrity or the firm's ambitions to protect the environment. The protection of workers' rights, on the other hand, is not only in the interest of the employees themselves, but also concerns NGOs and plays a crucial role in the media.[71] To disentangle the exact relation between CSR and

---

[68] This idea is also underlying the stakeholder approach to *strategic* management going back to Freeman (1984). For explicit references to the business case for CSR cf. Barnett (2007), pp. 795 et sqq.; Kurucz et al. (2008); Laszlo (2003); Benioff (2004); Paine (2003); Smith (2003), p. 58; SustainAbility (2006); Vogel (2005), pp. 16 et sqq. The Business Case is often also referred to as a *win–win* strategy, cf. Utting (2000), p. 20.

[69] Cf. footnote 109 on p. 29 and the literature cited there.

[70] Cf. Donaldson and Preston (1995); Mitchell et al. (1997); Rowley (1997); Berman et al. (1999); Hillman and Keim (2001); Graves and Waddock (2000); Harrisson and Freeman (1999); Ogden and Watson (1999); Ruf et al. (2001); Wood and Jones (1995).

[71] For instance, western consumers pay high attention to labour conditions in factories supplying textile marketers' such as Nike or Puma. Concerning negative media coverage consider the case of Siemens that had sold its mobile technology division to the Taiwan company Ben-Q. When the latter decided to close the German factories, Siemens was pushed by the public to take responsibility for workers that it legally did not employ anymore.

financial performance, it is useful to analyse which dimension of CSP might have a direct impact on what kind of mediating mechanism so that an indirect relation between social and financial performance might plausibly be assumed.

Identifying Distinct Effects of CSP and Its Single Dimensions

In an attempt to identify mechanisms that might mediate social and financial performance, one can first distinguish internal from external effects that take place inside or outside the organisation. From the various approaches that can be found in the literature and that will be presented later in detail, six such mechanisms prevail. These concern the internal areas of employees, operational efficiency and general management competencies, and the external issues customers, a firm's risk and its reputation on capital markets. Most of the arguments claiming positive impacts of CSP explain these effects by reference to social performance in general, but some also trace them back to single components of CSR such as fair labour standards or environmental performance. To hold these different arguments apart, the relation of the six mechanisms to (single components of) CSP is depicted by the following matrix (Fig. 3.6).

The vertical axis refers to a company's performance on single components of CSR and to its overall CSP, to which many authors attribute certain generic effects. The horizontal side lists the six aforementioned mechanisms that can typically be

Mechanisms	HR & Productivity (Employee Reputation)	Operational Efficiency (Reducing Waste of Resources)	Innovativeness/ General Mgt. Competencies	Customer Reputation	Risk Reduction	Reputation on Capital Markets
Components of CSP	**Internal**			**External**		
Over-all CSP (generic)						
Staff & Suppliers						
Society/ Community						
Corporate Governance & Business Ethics						
Customers/ Products						
Environmental Mgt.						

Fig. 3.6 Explaining a CSP/CFP-link through indirect mechanisms

found in the literature and that stand in direct connection with CSR on the one hand and financial performance on the other. Even though it is not useful to assume that each of these mechanisms is affected by every single CSR component, this matrix offers a frame of reference for generating hypotheses concerning their effects on financial performance.

Most of the arguments championing the business case for CSR attribute its positive effects to over-all CSP (*crr*)[72] as a generic competence. Concerning factors inside the organisation, substantial conceptual and empirical work has been devoted to the effects that CSR might have on *employee behaviour*. The essential claim is that a company's overall reputation with regards to CSR helps it recruit skilled people, retain them and reduce turnover. That in turn lowers recruiting and training costs, keeps motivation, productivity and loyalty high and thus has a positive impact on firm performance.[73] A different argument, typically brought forward from the perspective of the resource-based view, claims that proactive CSR management also affects *managerial as well as organisational competencies* in general.[74] These competences enable companies to be more responsive and to better react to new threats and opportunities in the organisational environment and thus to gain competitive advantages.[75]

In addition to such internal effects, a positive impact of a firm's CSP is often explained with reference to external factors. One of them is the company's *Customer Reputation* that is claimed to be influenced by a firm's efforts to address social and environmental issues. A firm's CSR activities might be positively (negatively) perceived by customers and increase (lower) their confidence and therefore their willingness to buy certain products and to pay premium prices.[76] While there are claims that a good CSR record can negatively influence a company's reputation,[77] several empirical studies suggest that there is a large number of customers that expects firms to behave socially responsible *and* that is willing to take their

---

[72] Throughout this section, variable names will be given in parentheses behind the full description. For an overview of all variables in use, cf. the appendix.

[73] Cf. Albinger and Freeman (2000); Backhaus et al. (2002); Greening and Turban (2000); McWilliams and Siegel (2001), p. 122; Peterson (2004); Riordan et al. (1997); Smith (2003), pp. 59–60; Turban and Greening (1997); Montgomery and Ramus (2003). For a critical assessment questioning these assumed effects, see Vogel (2005), pp. 56–59.

[74] Barney (1991); Hart (1995); Orlitzky et al. (2003), pp. 406–407; Wernerfelt (1984).

[75] Porter and Kramer (2006).

[76] Becker-Olsen et al. (2006); Du et al. (2007); Klein and Dawar (2004); Luo and Bhattacharya (2006); Murray and Vogel (1997), p. 155; Salmones et al. (2005); Smith (2003), pp. 60 sqq.

[77] Schwaiger (2004) distinguishes the two reputational dimensions 'sympathy' and 'competence' and finds that CSR has a positive relation with the 'sympathy' component but a negative one with 'competence'. Concerning *adverse* effects of a company's CSR efforts on reputation, see also Sen and Bhattacharya (2001).

purchase decisions in accordance with these expectations.[78] The question remains, however, whether this willingness effectively leads to *de facto* altered consumption patterns. It is evident that certain companies' success and the existence of entire markets are for a large part due to their positive image with regards to ethical issues.[79] But there are serious doubts that there is generally a fraction of ethically influenced consumers big enough to have a financial impact, so that there might be either no general link between CSR and consumer behaviour at all or only under certain, very special conditions.[80] A second external effect concerns the relation between a company's social performance and its *risk profile.* According to this argument, good CSP involving proactive stakeholder management often increases awareness for and lowers the risk of possibly negative effects such as NGO campaigns, consumer boycotts, government regulation, labour unrest, negative media coverage, etc.[81] The fact that creditors increasingly include CSR issues in their risk assessment procedures is an indicator for the correctness of this argument. Finally, a company's overall CSR engagement might considerably influence its *reputation on capital markets.* The constantly growing number and size of socially responsible investment (SRI) funds could have an influence on the behaviour of those companies that are in search of new capital and are therefore trying to act in line with the preferences of the capital market.[82] However, in the light of the relatively small importance of those funds that include ethical criteria into their investment decisions, the overall effect of CSR on capital markets can be questioned. Even though CSR does matter to some investors under some circumstances, in comparison to the financial performance of most firms, it can also be said to have only very little importance.[83]

To summarise, it is very unlikely that a clear positive or negative relation exists between a company's over-all social and its financial performance. First, as the above mentioned arguments show, there are as many arguments for the existence of such a link as there are doubts that actually lead to a denial of such a relation. Second, the argument developed in Sect. 2.3.1 still applies: the mediating mechanisms can only be explained in a differentiated analysis with reference to single components' effects on CFP. This leads to the following hypothesis:

H_{1a}: There is no measurable positive or negative relation between the *oekom research* over-all CSP grade (variable *crr*) and the respective firm's *Tobin's Q*.

Besides the arguments discussed earlier, each of the identified mechanisms can be affected not only by CSP in general but by the single CSR components that

78 Branco and Rodriguez (2006); Brammer and Pavlin (2004); Cryer and Ross (1997); Maignan (2001); Mohr et al. (2001); Schuler and Cording (2006). For theoretical analyses including such preferences in the consumer's utility function, see Bagnoli and Watts (2003) and Baron (2006b).

79 Vogel (2005), pp. 40–44.

80 Sen and Bhattacharya (2001); Vogel (2005), p. 48.

81 Branco and Rodriguez (2006); Fombrum et al. (2000); Heal (2005), pp. 8–9; Husted (2005), p. 176; Orlitzky and Benjamin (2001); Smith (2003), p. 60. For theoretical models including such mechanisms, see Baron (2001) and Baron (2006b).

82 Baron (2006a); Smith (2003), p. 63–64.

83 Vogel (2005), p. 70. See Teoh and Shiu (1990) for empirical support of this argument.

concern certain stakeholders, as discussed in Sect. 3.1.1.4. The literature on financial consequences of CSP investments also contains more differentiated arguments referring to these components' effects on certain internal and external mechanisms.

Considering a company's social performance with regards to Staff and Suppliers (*staff*), the most obvious direct effect is that on *HR and employee productivity*. Some empirical studies trace the aforementioned positive effects back to certain employment practices rather than to CSP in general. The idea is that employees are most satisfied with social expenditures concerning themselves rather than with charitable contributions outside the company.[84] A good relation with employees therefore has positive effects on the organisation's *operational efficiency*.[85] *Customer Reputation* is mostly affected by scandals that include bad working conditions in suppliers' production sites. As examples in the textile industry show, customers do care about how the products they buy are being produced. And they do hold the selling company responsible even though violations of human rights happen in factories that legally do not belong to the company finally selling the products.[86] Such customer reactions pose a risk on many companies, which explains why different kinds of management standards for social accounting and auditing have been developed and employed to mitigate these risks.[87] Taken together, these arguments lead to the following hypothesis:

H_{1b}: There is a positive link between performance along the staff and suppliers dimension (variable *staff*) and *Tobin's Q*.

As described earlier, the component Society and Community (*soc*) concerns issues such as charitable contributions and the relation with the community in which the company is operating. Internally, instruments such as sponsoring of cultural and sports events or cause-related marketing could turn into a competitive advantage by improving employee morale and boosting productivity (*HR and Productivity*).[88] Moreover, customers perceive these activities and could thereby be positively influenced in their perception of the company.[89] But, as Strahilevitz and Myers (1998) point out, the effectiveness of such measures cannot be equally expected across all industries but rather depends on specific factors such as the kind of product that is being sold.

With its capacity to build trust and confidence, a good relation to external stakeholders in the society and the community acts as an insurance against negative reactions when bad corporate acts occur. Consequently, corporate charitable contributions can also be seen as a means of *risk reduction*.[90] Finally, such activities are

---

[84] Branco and Rodriguez (2006), p. 121; SustainAbility (2006), p. 27.

[85] Pruzan (1998); SustainAbility (2006), p. 19.

[86] As an example, consider the development of *Nike*'s posture towards labour standards in manufacturing companies described in Vogel (2005), pp. 77–82.

[87] See for instance the social standards SA 8000 (developed by New-York based *Social Accounting International*) or AA 1000 (developed by the English NGO *AccountAbility*).

[88] SustainAbility (2006), p. 27; Porter and Kramer (2002).

[89] Fombrum and Shanley (1990); Smith and Alcorn (1991).

[90] Godfrey (2005), p. 786; Peloza (2006).

capable of positively influencing *reputation on capital markets*.[91] As Graff Zivin and Small (2005) show, this is not unconditionally true, though. In their theoretical model, they understand shares in responsible companies (i.e. those that make charitable contributions) as a charity-investment. Corporate 'altruism' in the form of donations is shown to only maximise firm valuation if a sizable fraction of investors prefer corporate philanthropy over direct charitable giving. Considering the low share of SRI funds compared to traditional ones, it is far from clear that the fraction is large enough in reality.

In sum, one cannot expect a definite relationship between society and community engagement and financial performance. First, as described earlier, the scores from *oekom research* were dichotomised for this study to allow comparisons across industries. This way, analyses can be carried out over a variety of industries, but render industry-specific analyses infeasible (with the exception of one industry class-specific interaction effect discussed in Sect. 2.1.2). Taking into account that many of the arguments above emphasise that positive effects cannot be expected unconditionally across industries, it is unlikely that a relation can be shown in this study. Second, it is not entirely clear whether the assumptions underlying the model of Graff Zivin and Small (2005) are met in reality. Therefore, it should be questioned that the possibly positive effects of a good performance along the component *Society and Community* are relevant in a statistical sense, which is captured in the following hypothesis:

H_{1c}: There is either a positive or no measurable relation between *oekom research*'s assessment of a company's relation with society and community (variable *soc*) and *Tobin's Q*.

Since the component Corporate Governance and Business Ethics (*corpgov*) comprises shareholder-related topics (transparency of compensation schemes, independence of the board, shareholder democracy, etc.), there are large parallels to the finance literature research strand analysing the link between corporate governance and financial performance. Such a link is mainly established via the *capital market*'s reaction to a firm's ability/failure to meet the standards set by mostly national corporate governance codes. Empirical evidence concerning this link has been mixed so far. On the one hand, a number of studies found a positive relation to market-based performance data.[92] On the other hand, several works could not confirm such a link. In their empirical study of German companies, Nowak et al. (2005) come to the conclusion that voluntary compliance with or the failure to adhere to the corporate governance codex does neither positively nor negatively affect firm valuation on capital markets. Core et al. (2006) find a negative relation between their corporate governance index and market evaluation.

But *corpgov* does not only refer to classical corporate governance issues but also to the company's efforts to ensure fair business practices through codes of conduct and similar management systems. Their aim is to effectively prevent malpractices

[91] Lev et al. (2006).

[92] See Gompers et al. (2003) for US-stockmarkets; Bauer et al. (2004) for European companies; Black et al. (2006) for Korean companies; and Drobetz et al. (2004) for Germany.

such as price collusion, corruption and the like. If for instance a company is involved in controversies or even has been found guilty of breaking the law, this leads to a downgrade of the rating within this component. Since such scandals have proven to influence *consumer behaviour* and *employee morale*,[93] the grade used by *oekom research* data should in sum have significant effects on financial performance. This leads to the next hypothesis:

H_{1d}: There is a positive influence of activities included in the component Corporate Governance and Business Ethics (variable *corpgov*) on *Tobin's Q*.

Activities associated with the Customers and Product Responsibility (*cust*) component should mostly influence customer reputation. The component includes classical Customer Relation Management (CRM) issues such as service and transparency, but also social and environmental features of the activities along the value-creation chain (products in use, genetically modified food, product safety, pollution, etc.). Classical CRM elements have repeatedly proven to influence customer satisfaction and can therefore be expected to have a positive impact on financial performance.[94] Moreover, environmentally and ethically responsible products often imply the possibility to enter new markets where extra-prices can be charged. This especially applies to environmental product features that lead to differentiation in the market.[95] The question is of course which role these relatively small markets play in general. For example, the theoretical model of Arora and Gangopadhyay (1995) suggests that environmental over-compliance only pays within a very limited fraction of the market that is willing to pay premium prices. Interestingly in this context, empirical investigations have failed to unambiguously prove the asserted positive relation. Brown and Dacin (1997) for instance cannot find a clear link between product responsibility and product evaluation.

Since the variable used concerns a variety of product- and customer-related aspects and since the majority of studies assumes a positive consumer awareness, it should in sum be expected to have an impact on customer behaviour.

H_{1e}: There is a positive relation between Customer and Product Responsibility (variable *cust*) on the one side and *Tobin's Q* on the other.

The question of whether Environmental Management and Eco-Efficiency (*enman*) is able to gain benefits that outweigh its costs is one of the most intensively scrutinised in the business and society literature. It concerns all of the aforementioned mediating mechanisms, which allow environmentally friendly companies to gain competitive advantages.[96] The *HR and Productivity* argument for instance also applies to this issue, as employees increasingly care for the environmental performance of their company in times when environmental concerns (scarcity of resources, climatic change, environmental pollution, etc.) play a growing role in society, politics and media.[97] Firms often aim at reorganising their business

[93] SustainAbility (2006), p. 27–30.

[94] Anderson et al. (1994); Anderson et al. (2004); Mithas et al. (2005); Morgan and Hunt (1994).

[95] Flaherty and Raaport (1991); Hart (1995); Utting (2000), pp. 20–21.

[96] Klassen and McLaughlin (1996); Klassen and Whybark (1999); Porter and van der Linde (1995).

[97] Bauer and Aiman-Smith (1996); SustainAbility (2006) p. 27.

activities so that supply-, production- and distribution-procedures are optimised in efficient ways concerning the use of resources and the production of waste.[98] These product- and process-related attempts are often not only employed because of ethical considerations but because they are expected to come along with gains in *operational efficiency*[99] and general competencies such as *innovativeness*.[100]

Clearly, the effects of environmental performance are not restricted to internal mechanisms but also imply external impacts. The effects concerning *Customer Reputation* via product differentiation are mainly captured by the variable 'Customer and Product Responsibility', but environmentally friendly production and distribution processes can effectively lead to *risk reduction*, for instance by earning legitimacy in the view of external stakeholders or avoiding external regulation (e.g. by the SEC or regional governments).[101] Also, *capital markets* have proven to be a powerful driver of effective environmental management as they provide incentives for companies to implement 'green' technologies. One argument is that capital markets penalise companies that produce negative externalities and thus social costs. This way, companies may be forced to lower their pollution level if the gains of these changes outweigh the benefits of polluting.[102] Additionally, when assessing a company's credibility, not only banks as creditors but also investment funds increasingly take into account firm environmental performance, which influences its cost of capital.[103] In their theoretical model, Heinkel et al. (2001) show that SRI screening strategies ('green investment') can lead to higher costs of capital of heavy polluting companies and consequently force them to implement environmentally friendlier strategies and technologies. Their result, however, is restricted to the case in which there are enough screening funds (approximately 20% of the market) to effectively put pressure on companies.

As the discussion shows, the majority of theoretical and empirical work on the effects of environmental performance suggests that its benefits are larger than its costs. This result is reflected in the following hypothesis:

> H_{1f}: There is a positive correlation between Environmental Management and Eco-Efficiency (variable *enman*) and *Tobin's Q*.

Tracing Causality: The Direction of the CSP/CFP-Link

At this point, it is important to address an issue which has so far been faded out, but which will be relevant to the following statistical analyses due to technical reasons.

---

[98] Ball et al. (2005); Hart (1995); Russo and Fouts (1997).

[99] Branco and Rodriguez (2006); Dowell et al. (2000); Heal (2005), p. 9; Orsato (2006), p. 131; Porter and van der Linde (1995); SustainAbility (2006), p. 19; Utting (2000), p. 20.

[100] SustainAbility (2006), p. 31; Russo and Fouts (1997).

[101] Bansal and Clelland (2004); Maxwell et al. (2000); Spicer (1978b); SustainAbility (2006), p. 29.

[102] Heal (2005), pp. 12–16.

[103] SustainAbility (2006), p. 21.

Up to now, all arguments have only concerned one direction of causality: they have analysed the consequences that certain components of CSR are expected to have on distinct mechanisms, which in turn have positive effects on financial performance. This is not the only conceivable relational direction, though. As has been often mentioned in the literature, two types of a causational relation between CSP and CFP can be conceived of. The first explanation for why such a relation might exist has been labelled the 'good management' approach.[104] According to this argument superior CSR as well as financial performance are both a function of good management. This is in line with the mechanisms identified so far. The second and hitherto ignored argument for why there might be a correlation assumes a different causal relation and has been coined the 'slack resources' hypothesis. It essentially assumes that management only considers ethical causes beyond compliance if there are enough resources that allow for such expenditures (this argument becomes particularly evident in the case of charitable donations). From this perspective, good social performance is seen to be a function of prior financial success.

Although both arguments describe very different interdependencies, they are not mutually exclusive. After all, it is plausible to assume both directions and thus simultaneous causality between social and financial performance.[105] As will become clear later, the empirical model chosen implicitly assumes only one causal direction, which involves econometric problems that will be addressed separately.[106]

3.3.1.2 Interaction Effects

The discussion in Sect. 2.3 showed that even though there are good reasons to assume the existence of certain kinds of a CSP/CFP-link, it is not plausible to assume such links universally and unconditionally. A company's exposure to stakeholder pressure, its industry, the degree of internationalisation and firm age are all examples of contingencies that could influence the relation between social and financial performance. In the context of linear regression analyses, such conditions can best be modelled by interaction terms. When two variables interact with each other, the level of one variable influences the effect of an explanatory variable on the dependent variable.[107] To give an example in the context of this study, the financial gains from superior environmental management and eco-efficiency are presumably larger in heavy-polluting industries (e.g. Oil and Gas) than in the financial industries such as Banking and Financials. This is because there are higher reputational effects to cause, higher potential cost cuts, etc.

To include such relations, the interaction terms will be constructed by multiplying the moderator with the respective CSP variable. However, including many

---

[104] Concerning this distinction, see Orlitzky et al. (2003), p. 406; Ullman (1985) and Waddock and Graves (1997), p. 306.

[105] Recall, however, that the empirical analysis of CSP drivers in Sect. 3.2.3 does not lend support to this argument.

[106] Cf. Sect. 3.3.3.3.

[107] Gujarati (2003), pp. 310–312; Stock and Watson (2007), pp. 277–290.

interaction effects with dummy variables bears the risk of having to small sample sizes that would prevent the calculations of regression coefficients by OLS. Therefore, only the most important interaction effects will be considered.

To capture the idea that industries with a high environmental impact have more to win (lose) from good (bad) environmental performance, *oekom research*'s industry classification is used. This scheme differentiates four different industry classes, which are represented by the binary variable *class* taking value 1 if the company belongs to one of the two industries with the highest impact (industries III and IV) and value 0 otherwise.[108]

$$class = \begin{cases} 1, & \text{if industry III, IV} \\ 0, & \text{otherwise.} \end{cases}$$

Multiplying this term with *enman* gives the (dummy) interaction term, the coefficient of which will finally measure by how much the effect of *enman* on *Tobin's Q* is higher for companies in high-polluting industries than for others. This is summarised in the following hypothesis:

H_{2a}: The influence of Environmental Management and Eco-Efficiency (variable *enman*) on *Tobin's Q* will be significantly higher in heavy polluting industries (variable *class*).

A second moderator of the CSP/CFP-link is firm visibility, which is closely related to the company's scrutiny by the critical public.[109] This exposure especially concerns the prevention or at least mitigation of negative effects in the case of scandals that are prevalent with regards to environmental pollution and issues that evoke morally motivated reactions such as human rights violation and corruption issues. In this context it can be stated that larger firms are generally more visible in the public and are therefore more vulnerable to NGO pressure, consumer boycotts, etc. This relation is captioned by the following three hypotheses:

H_{2b}: The influence of Environmental Management and Eco-Efficiency (variable *enman*) on *Tobin's Q* will be significantly higher for companies with a relatively high visibility (variable *size*).

H_{2c}: The influence of Staff and Suppliers (variable *staff*) on *Tobin's Q* will be significantly higher for companies with a relatively high visibility (variable *size*).

H_{2d}: The influence of Corporate Governance and Business Ethics (variable *corpgov*) on *Tobin's Q* will be significantly higher for companies with a relatively high visibility (variable *size*).

Table 3.8 provides an overview of all hypotheses developed in this chapter. Via the discussion of possible mechanisms mediating between CSP components on the one hand and financial performance on the other, it was argued that parts of the single components are expected to have an influence on *Tobin's Q*. No such relation should be expected concerning the overall CSP, however. Four interaction terms operationalise contingencies upon which possible CSP/CFP-links are expected to depend.

---

[108] For *oekom*'s industry classification, cf. Fig. 3.2 on page 36.

[109] Smith (2003), p. 60.

Table 3.8 Hypotheses for the cross-sectional OLS regression model

Summary of hypotheses regarding the influence of explanatory variables on Tobin's Q				
Category	Variable name	Full name	Expected influence	Hypothesis
CSP variables	*crr*	Corporate responsibility rating	None	H_{1a}
	staff	Staff and suppliers	Positive	H_{1b}
	soc	Society and community	Positive/none	H_{1c}
	corpgov	Corporate governance and business ethics	Positive	H_{1d}
	cust	Customer and product responsibility	Positive	H_{1e}
	enman	Environmental management and eco-efficiency	Positive	H_{1f}
Interaction effects	*enman* × *class*	Environmental management and eco-efficiency × pollution class	Positive	H_{2a}
	enman × *size*	Environmental management and eco-efficiency × company size	Positive	H_{2b}
	staff × *size*	Staff and suppliers × company size	Positive	H_{2c}
	corpgov × *size*	Corporate governance and business ethics × company size	Positive	H_{2d}

3.3.2 Cross-Sectional Regression Analysis

3.3.2.1 The OLS-Model

To test the hypotheses developed in the previous section, three Models are specified according to the discussion above. In each case, *Tobin's Q* is regressed on a set of CSP variables and the control variables. The first model includes only the overall CSP-variable, the others contain the single CSP component variables. To control for effects on firm performance that cannot be attributed to differences in CSP and in line with previous studies using *Tobin's Q*, the firm's market risk (CAPM's Beta),[110]

[110] Waddock and Graves (1997).

its debt-to-equity ratio (leverage)[111] and its size[112] measured by annual sales will be included as control variables. To test whether the group-wise inclusion of the interaction terms significantly adds to the explained variance, the second and third models are computed without and with the interaction terms, respectively. Stated formally, the three following equations capture these models:

$$Q = \beta_0 + \beta_1 crr + \beta_2 risk + \beta_3 lev + \beta_4 size + u^{113} \tag{5}$$

$$Q = \beta_0 + \beta_1 staff + \beta_2 soc + \beta_3 corpgov + \beta_4 cust + \beta_5 enman + \beta_6 risk + \beta_7 lev + \beta_8 size + u \tag{6}$$

$$Q = \beta_0 + \boldsymbol{\beta}\mathbf{x} + u, \tag{7}$$

where in (7), β_0 is the constant, $\boldsymbol{\beta}$ is the row vector for the coefficients of the regressors contained in the column vector $\mathbf{x}$ and u is an error term capturing stochastic influences on the dependent variable. The independent variables in $\mathbf{x}$ are:

x_1 through x_8, which are identical with (6)

$$\begin{aligned} x_9 &= class \\ x_{10} &= enman \times class \\ x_{11} &= enman \times size \\ x_{12} &= soc \times size \\ x_{13} &= corpgov \times size. \end{aligned}$$

The true regression coefficients in the population are estimated by Ordinary Least Squares (OLS) estimation using the data in the sample described earlier.

3.3.2.2 Test Results and Discussion

Table 3.9 contains the results of the cross-sectional regression analysis (OLS) regressing *Tobin's Q* on a set of CSP variables and controlling for *leverage*, *risk* and *size*. *Column (1)* shows that the beta-coefficient of the over-all CSP variable (*crr*) is positive but has a standard error so large that the influence cannot be considered to be significant. The null hypothesis stating that there is no influence of *crr* on *Tobin's Q* can thus not be rejected; this result is in line with H_{1a}.

The model testing the influence of distinct CSP variables on *Tobin's Q* is reported in *column (2)*. The F-statistic for the joint hypothesis that all coefficients are zero is $F(8{,}285) = 26.05$, so that this null hypothesis can be rejected on the 1% level (critical value: 2.57). The constant (intercept) gives the expected *Tobin's Q* of a firm for which all explanatory variables take value 0. That is, a company that performs low with respect to all CSP variables and displays average risk, size and leverage, is expected to have a *Tobin's Q* of approximately 1.5, meaning that the market value of the firm is 50% higher than its replacement costs. 44.31% (R^2) of variance in

[111] Dowell et al. (2000); McConnell and Servaes (1990); McWilliams and Siegel (2000).

[112] Claessens et al. (2002); Dowell et al. (2000); McConnell and Servaes (1990); Hillman and Keim (2001); Waddock and Graves (1997).

Table 3.9 Cross-sectional regression with *Tobin's Q* as the dependent variable

Results of the Multiple Linear Regression (OLS Estimation): Tobin's Q			
Model	(1)	(2)	(3)
Regressors			
crr	0.0745 (0.2770)		
staff		−0.0379 (0.6110)	−0.0519 (0.5190)
corpgov		0.1780** (0.0130)	0.1640** (0.0220)
enman		0.1947** (0.0190)	0.0758 (0.4210)
cust		−0.1412** (0.0500)	−0.1346* (0.0610)
soc		0.1127 (0.1100)	0.1379 (0.1100)
risk	−0.0579 (0.5350)	−0.1060 (0.2590)	−0.1064 (0.2540)
lev	−1.8178*** (0.0000)	−1.8294*** (0.0000)	−1.6684*** (0.0000)
size	−0.1141*** (0.0000)	−0.1096*** (0.0000)	−0.0790* (0.0740)
enman × *class*			0.2110* (0.0640)
enman × *size*			0.0108 (0.8560)
staff × *size*			0.0198 (0.7260)
corpgov × *size*			−0.1320** (0.0230)
Constant	1.6086*** (0.0000)	1.4938*** (0.0000)	1.4679*** (0.0000)
Summary statistics			
N	294	294	294
Prob > *F*	0.0000	0.0000	0.0000
R^2	0.4108	0.4431	0.4604
F(CSP); *F*(Int)		3.86***	1.82

Dependent variable: *Tobin's Q*. *p*-values ($P > t$) are reported in parentheses (calculated with heteroscedasticity-robust standard errors). Individual coefficients are statistically significant at the *10%, **5% or ***1% level (two-tailed *t*-test). *F*(CSP) and *F*(Int) indicate the respective *F*-value to test the joint hypothesis that all CSP-variables (model 2) or interaction effects (model 3) equal zero after their groupwise inclusion (compared to the previous model, respectively)

Tobin's Q can be explained by the independent variables. To check whether this is not exclusively due to the control variables, the joint hypothesis that the group of CSP-variables equals zero is tested by means of an *F*-Test. The result rejects the null hypothesis on the 1% level, so that it is safe to conclude that the inclusion of the CSP variables adds explanatory power.

More precisely, three of the five CSP variables have a significant influence on the dependent variable. *corpgov* (Corporate Governance and Business Ethics) has an estimated coefficient of 0.1780. Since the CSP variables are dummy variables, this result means that – everything else being equal – companies in the high performing group have a *Tobin's Q*, which is in average by 0.1780 higher than that of those in the low performing group (i.e. the intercept of the regression function differs by that value from one group to the other). With a standard error of 0.0710, this coefficient is significant at the 5% level, that is, if the null hypothesis (*corpgov* has no influence) were true, the probability of receiving such a coefficient estimate would be lower than 5% so that the null hypothesis can be rejected on this level. The same arguments apply to the variable *enman* (Environmental Management and Eco-Efficiency), which has a positive coefficient of 0.1947 (significant at the 5% level), indicating that companies with a good environmental performance are valued higher in the market than others. The table also shows that *cust* (Customer and Product Responsibility) has a negative coefficient of −0.1412, which is significant at the 5% level. In contrast, there are no influences with respect to the components *staff* (Staff and Suppliers) and *soc* (Society and Community). A discussion of these (partly counter-intuitive) results will follow during the next chapter.

Column (3) reports the coefficients of the model including all interaction effects. The influence of *corpgov* and *cust* qualitatively remains the same, whereas the standard error of the *enman* coefficient increases so that the influence cannot be said to be significant anymore. The two significant interaction effects are those of *enman* × *class* (10%) and that of *corpgov* × *size* (5% level), indicating that the effects of *enman* and *corpgov* differ for companies of different industry classes and size. The positive coefficient of the interaction between *enman* and *class* suggests that for those companies in heavy polluting industries, the effect of good environmental performance is by approximately 20 percentage points higher than for the other industries. The interpretation of the coefficient of *corpgov* × *size* (−0.1320) is as follows: for company A that is 1% larger than company B, the expected effect of a change in *corpgov* from 0 to 1 is by $0.01 \times 0.132 = 0.00132$ lower (though still positive) than for company B (note that *size* are log-values). Although two of the interaction terms have significant coefficients, the null hypothesis that all of the interaction terms included in model (3) have coefficients of zero cannot be rejected by an F-test (p-value: 0.1260).[114]

For all three models, the control variables remain very similar what regards strength and sign. *lev* and *size* have a negative and significant effect on *Tobin's Q*, whereas risk has a negative but insignificant influence.

3.3.2.3 Discussion

To begin with the control variables, the estimated coefficient of *risk* needs explanation, since shareholders should expect higher financial returns from assets that are

[114] For the necessity of 'omnibus tests' in the context of interaction effects, see also Jaccard and Turrisi (2003), pp. 4–7.

riskier.[115] In spite of this theoretical argument, the relation between risk and return has repeatedly been shown to be negative or non-significant in empirical studies so that this result is consistent with earlier findings.[116] The gains and risks of the debt to equity ratio in corporate finance is a long-debated subject in finance theory, but the negative sign of the *lev* coefficient is congruent with past studies, where leverage and long-term debt have been shown to be negatively associated with measures of financial performance.[117] The negative coefficient of *size* measured by annual sales is also consistent with previous studies, where variables measuring size have been shown to have a negative influence on firm performance.[118]

Since model (1) shows no significant effect of *crr*, the null hypothesis that its coefficient equals zero cannot be rejected. This result lends support to hypothesis H_{1a} according to which there is no reason to assume a link between a company's financial performance and its social performance as long as the latter is operationalised by an aggregated over-all measure of CSP.

The positive and significant coefficients of *corpgov* and *enman* in model (2) support the arguments for hypotheses H_{1d} and H_{1f}, which predict a positive relation of these variables to *Tobin's Q*. According to the estimation reported in Table 3.9, firms belonging to the high performing group along the *corpgov* (*enman*) dimensions, in average, have a *Tobin's Q* which is 18 (19) percentage points higher than that of their reference group which was rated below the industry-mean. However, the influence of *enman* becomes insignificant due to the coefficient's increased standard error, as soon as interaction terms are included into the analysis, as shown in column (3).

In contrast to H_{1b} and H_{1c}, the null hypotheses stating that the coefficients of the variables *staff* and *soc* are zero, cannot be rejected on the basis of the sample. Statistically, variance in *Tobin's Q* can therefore not be ascribed to performance differences with regards to staff orientation and all those issues contained in the component *Society and Community*. This is surprising in the light of the arguments brought forward in Sect. "Identifying Distinct Effects of CSP and Its Single Dimensions" which suggested positive (negative) effects of superior (inferior) performance with respect to the company's own and its suppliers' employees. It has been questioned, however, whether these effects are high enough to trigger measurable effects across industries. It is sometimes even argued that the biggest boycotts only have a very small and temporary impact, if any.[119] The data set

[115] Concerning the foundations of the CAPM, see Sharpe (1964); Lintner (1965); Mossin (1966). For an empirical discussion, see Spremann (2003), pp. 253 et sqq.

[116] Cf. Hillman and Keim (2001). In a different context, Elsas (2003) shows that in a standard OLS setting the relation between risk and return is flat. For an in-depth discussion of the empirical risk-/return relation, see Bowman (1980); Henkel (2000).

[117] Cf. Dowell et al. (2000), p. 1067; Morck et al. (1988), pp. 300 and 309; Waddock and Graves (1997). The theoretical discussion on the optimal capital structure mainly centers around the assumptions of perfect or imperfect capital markets. For a discussion of the main arguments in that context, cf. Brealey and Myers (2003), pp. 465–515.

[118] Claessens et al. (2002); Dowell et al. (2000); Gorton and Schmid (2000); Hillman and Keim (2001); McConnell and Servaes (1990); Waddock and Graves (1997).

[119] Vogel (2005), pp. 51–53.

used for this study apparently fails to support the existence of such effects. The same applies to the component *Society and Community*. One possible explanation for the non-significant coefficient of *soc* is that although companies spend much money on charitable causes, they do not do so in the 'proper' way. As Porter and Kramer (2002) argue, most company's charitable giving is not strategic in a sense that it manages to combine the company's specific competencies with philanthropic projects that have a social impact. Therefore, many companies fail to benefit from the potentially positive effects of charitable contributions. Another explanation would be that data from *oekom research* are performance-based and not perception-based. It is not clear whether the consumers' and other external stakeholders' perceptions of a firm's performance are identical. So even if a company's performance is very good judged on the basis of accountable data, the firm might fail to communicate this performance effectively.

The most surprising result of the regression analysis is the negative sign of the *cust* coefficient, suggesting that firms with a comparably bad rating on *Customer and Product Responsibility* outperform those with a good rating by an average of 14.12 percentage points in *Tobin's Q*. The arguments reflected in H_{1e} would have predicted the opposite effect. The idea was that especially customers would reward ethically desirable product features, which would allow for higher prices in certain markets. As mentioned during that discussion, this argument might be restricted to certain industries, presumably to those of consumer markets. This might also be an explanation for why previous studies have failed to support the assumption of a positive relation between product features and financial performance.[120] It should also be noted that the *cust* coefficent does not significantly deviate from zero when the dependent variable is replaced by the accounting measure return on equity (cf. the robustness checks in the following chapter).

Since two of the four interaction terms have no significant regression coefficients and since the F-Test could not reject the hypothesis that all of them equal zero, the results of the study fail to lend full support for hypotheses H_{2a} through H_{2d}. In contrast to these hypotheses, the results derived from the empirical analysis do not clearly depend on the factors *class* and *size*. Although the positive coefficient of the *enman* $\times$ *class* interaction term would suggest that especially companies in heavy-polluting industries can benefit from environmentally friendly strategies, the result of the joint F-Test cannot rule out that these effects are random.

The negative coefficient of the interaction term *corpgov* $\times$ *size* is puzzling as well, as it contradicts H_{2d}. Apparently, positive effects of good corporate governance have been more effective within smaller firms, so that the statistical relation between firm size and *corpgov* becomes smaller with increasing firm size.

---

[120] See Brown and Dacin (1997).

3.3.3 *Robustness of the Model*

3.3.3.1 Regression Diagnosis

Ordinary Least Squares (OLS) estimation is a powerful tool to estimate a linear function capturing the relationship between one dependent and several independent variables. Given the correctness of certain assumptions, OLS is the best linear unbiased estimator (BLUE) of the true regression coefficients conditional on the value of the regressors. These conditions are specified by the Gauss–Markov properties that have to hold for OLS to be the BLUE.[121] Therefore, each of these assumptions is tested for applicability in the context of this study. The requirements can best be discussed for the general linear regression equation

$$y = \beta_0 + \boldsymbol{\beta}\mathbf{x} + u,$$

where y is the dependent variable to be explained, β_0 is a constant term, $\mathbf{x}$ the vector of regressors and $\boldsymbol{\beta}$ the vector of their slope coefficients. u represents an error term capturing all (stochastic) influences on y, which are not explained by the constant and the regressors.

The first condition states that, given the vector of explanatory variables $\mathbf{x}$, the error term in the linear regression has a conditional mean of zero, or stated formally: $E(u|\mathbf{x}) = 0$. This condition also implies that all influences on the dependent variable that are contained in u are unrelated with $\mathbf{x}$, that is $\text{cov}(u, \mathbf{x}) = 0$. If this assumption is violated, the variable correlated with the error term is considered to be an endogenous variable, and the OLS estimator of the regression coefficient is biased and inconsistent.[122] The correctness of this assumption cannot be tested formally but there are several common sources of violation, which will be checked for plausibility in the following.[123] To avoid *non-linearity*, all categorically scaled CSP ratings were transformed into binary variables. Furthermore, log values of sales were taken for the *size* variable, because percentage changes can be assumed to have constant marginal effects. To mitigate the problem of biases and inconsistent estimators due to *omitted variables*, the commonly used control variables were included in the regression model. *Measurement errors* in the CSP variables have been tried to avoid by using the best available data for the assessment of a company's social performance.[124] A severe source of endogeneity is the possibly *simultaneous causality* between the independent variable (here: *Tobin's Q*) and (some of) the regressors

---

[121] Cf. Stock and Watson (2007), pp. 126–131 and 168; see also Gujarati (2003), pp. 65–76.

[122] This argument will be formally discussed in Sect. 3.3.3.3. Throughout this work, the term 'endogenous' refers to variables being correlated with the error term in the regression equation. It does *not* refer to the dependent variable, which is sometimes called the endogenous variable in other works.

[123] For the most common sources of endogeneity, see Stock and Watson (2007), pp. 316–327.

[124] For the discussion of the quality of *oekom research* data and the comparison to those of KLD, cf. Sects. 3.1.1.1 through 3.1.1.3.

(here: CSP variables). As was argued before and will be discussed in Sect. 3.3.3.3, this is a problem applying to this study which needs to be addressed separately.

The second condition considers the relation between the sample and the underlying population and requires that all observations must be drawn from the population by simple random sampling, so that $(\mathbf{x}, y)$ are independently and identically distributed (i.i.d.). Although the independence of the variables is mostly a problem within panel data and time series analysis, the question remains whether the sample drawn is random. Because of the following selection problems, randomness might be a critical point in this study. Since *oekom research* sells its assessments to institutional investors, it only rates publicly traded companies, which are not comparable to other firms with respect to various characteristics (such as size, profitability, management's shareholder value orientation, etc.). Second, the study uses only a sub-sample of the research spectrum because of differences in the rating methodology.[125] To correct for possible sample biases, one would need information on the companies that are not in the sample, what regards the explanatory variables. This information is of course not available, otherwise it could be included in the analysis. Since it is not clear whether the selection is random, and since selection biases cannot be accounted for in this study, the results only apply to major publicly traded companies and are not automatically transferable to privately owned mid-sized or small enterprises.

Third, large outliers have to be unlikely, that is x and y have non-zero finite fourth moments. As became clear through the descriptive statistics in Sect. 3.1, this assumption is not violated. Condition four requires that there is no perfect multicollinearity, that is the independent variables are not perfectly correlated with each other. A common measure of multicollinearity is the Variance Inflation Factor (VIF), which should be below 10.[126] A test for models (1) through (3) reveals that the VIF range from 1.09 to 3.62 so that these numbers are well below the critical value.

The fifth assumption states that the error terms must be homoscedastic, that is the variance of the error term conditional on the regressors is constant: $\text{var}(u|\mathbf{x}) = \sigma_u^2$. A Breusch–Pagan test for heteroscedasticity rejected the null hypothesis of homoscedasticity on the 1% significance level for all models.[127] Consequently, all models were estimated with heteroscedasticity-robust standard errors according to White (1980) in order to still obtain consistent estimates.

3.3.3.2 Market-Data Vs. Accounting-Data for Financial Performance

To see how sensitive the results obtained are to changes in the measurement of financial performance, the four models described earlier are tested with an accounting measure as the independent variable. Therefore, the analysis from Sect. 3.3.2 is

---

125 Cf. footnote 177. These other companies are less demanded by the relevant institutional investors and are therefore not rated with the same in-depth methodology.

126 Cf. Hair et al. (2006), pp. 230.

127 Breusch and Pagan (1979).

Table 3.10 Cross-sectional regression with *roe* as the dependent variable

Results of the multiple linear regression (OLS estimation): roe_{2006}			
Model	(1)	(2)	(3)
Regressors			
crr	0.1390		
	(0.8920)		
staff		−0.9445	−1.5291
		(0.4080)	(0.1890)
corpgov		2.1526**	1.9685*
		(0.0370)	(0.0520)
enman		2.5669**	−0.7447
		(0.0410)	(0.6060)
cust		−1.5748	−1.3440
		(0.1320)	(0.1840)
soc		−0.7445	−0.2914
		(0.5450)	(0.8110)
risk	0.7074	0.3098	0.6759
	(0.5740)	(0.8060)	(0.5850)
lev	1.1498	1.1119	4.7237**
	(0.5840)	(0.5890)	(0.0450)
size	1.1573***	1.3239***	2.0323***
	(0.0090)	(0.0040)	(0.0030)
enman × *class*			5.8784***
			(0.0000)
enman × *size*			−1.0595
			(0.2940)
staff × *size*			0.2701
			(0.7850)
corpgov × *size*			−1.5429*
			(0.0740)
Constant	17.1485***	16.5735***	16.4514***
	(0.0000)	(0.0000)	(0.0000)
Summary statistics			
N	294	294	294
Prob > *F*	0.0362	0.0111	0.0000
R^2	0.0329	0.0641	0.1233
F(CSP); *F*(Int)		1.83*	4.72***

Dependent variable: roe_{2006}. *p*-values ($P > t$) are reported in parentheses (calculated with heteroscedasticity-robust standard errors). Individual coefficients are statistically significant at the *10%, **5% or ***1% level (two-tailed *t*-test). *F*(CSP) and *F*(Int) indicate the respective *F*-value to test the joint hypothesis that all CSP-variables (model 2) or interaction effects (model 3) equal zero after their groupwise inclusion (compared to the previous model, respectively)

repeated by regressing return on equity (*roe*) on the CSP and control variables of the previous sections.

Table 3.10 reports the result of the OLS regression using return on equity as the dependent variable. The coefficients of the control variables change with respect to the effects of *lev* and *size*, whereas β_{risk} is still insignificant. *size* is now significantly positive (formerly negative) throughout all three models, suggesting that larger firms operate more efficiently, financial performance being measured by accounting data. *lev* has insignificant coefficients with the exception of column (3) that includes interaction terms.

As before, model (1), which captures social performance with only one aggregated CSP variable, does not show any significant influence of CSP on financial performance. Model (2) including the single CSP components reveals similar results compared to Table 3.9. As before, *staff* and *soc* are insignificant and therefore fail to explain variance in the dependent variable. Again the variable *cust* has a negative coefficient which, however, is not a statistically significant result. The *enman* and *corpgov* coefficients are both positive and significant on the 5% level as before, and so their interpretation remains unaltered as well. The joint hypothesis that all CSP variables equal zero is rejected on the 10% level, which suggests that the reported results are not random.

Comparable to the regression using *Tobin's Q* as the dependent variable, the results change after including the interaction terms in model (3). The coefficient of *enman* becomes insignificant and the significantly positive interaction term *enman* × *class* can be interpreted as support for the hypothesis that a positive relation between environmental and financial performance can only be expected if *class* takes value 1. The result with respect to the surprisingly negative coefficient of *corpgov* × *size* remains unaltered. In contrast to the previous regression reported in Table 3.9, the F-Test now suggests that the group-wise inclusion of interaction term adds explanatory power to the model so that the interaction effects cannot be assumed to be randomly different from zero.

In sum, the results as regards CSP are relatively robust to a substitution of the market-based measure of financial performance by an accounting-based measure. Both regressions suggest that relatively high ratings on the CSR components *Environmental Management and Eco-Efficiency* as well as on *Corporate Governance and Business Ethics* are positively related to financial performance. With respect to environmental performance, this positive correlation is stronger in or even restricted to the case of companies in high-polluting industries. In contrast to that, the effect of *corpgov* becomes smaller with increasing firm size.

3.3.3.3 Simultaneous Causality as a Source of Endogeneity

So far, the empirical analysis has aimed at explaining the effect of CSP on financial performance. As shown in Sect. "Tracing Causality: The Direction of the CSP/CFP-Link", this is not the only conceivable direction of causality, though. It is also possible to assume that especially those companies engage in CSR activities (and therefore receive high ratings) that are financially successful and can thus afford expenditures for high environmental production standards, social causes and the like. In that case, causality would run from financial to social performance. This simultaneous causality between the dependent variable (here: financial performance) and some independent variables (here: CSP variables) leads to the econometric problem of endogeneity and thus violates a central assumption of OLS estimation.

Although simultaneous causality has been a well-known problem in empirical CSR research for a long time,[128] it has very rarely been properly addressed as a source of endogeneity that leads to inconsistent estimates.[129] This is rather surprising, given that the problem is commonly addressed in corporate governance research, which is arguable a similar topic.[130] The analysis of determinants of CSP in Sect. 3.2 failed to support the assumption that past financial performance helps explain CSP. Nevertheless, previous studies have found a positive influence[131] and so the possibility of a reverse causality needs to be taken into account. What follows is a formal explanation for why simultaneous causality poses a problem on OLS estimation before the subsequent section will discuss possibilities to technically address this problem.

As shown earlier, the first OLS assumption is the independence of the residuals conditional on the regressors, which in the case of single linear regression means that $E(u|x) = 0$, in our case implying that $\text{cov}(x,u) = 0$.[132] Under this assumption, the OLS estimator for the regression coefficient is consistent because it can be shown to have the probability limit $\hat{\beta}_1 \xrightarrow{p} \beta_1 + \rho_{xu}\frac{\sigma_u}{\sigma_x}$.[133] That is, if the covariance between the error term and the regressor is zero, the estimated regression coefficient converges in probability to the true coefficient, and so the OLS estimator of the regression coefficient is consistent. If, however, $\text{cov}(x,u) \neq 0$, the assumption is violated and the estimator for β_1 is not consistent anymore, because it over/underestimates the true coefficient by $\rho_{xu}\frac{\sigma_u}{\sigma_x} \neq 0$, even if the sample size is very large. Thus, endogeneity leads to inconsistent estimates.

One source of endogeneity is simultaneous causality as it leads to a correlation between the regressor and the error term. This can best be shown for the simple case of only one regressor. Since there is not only an influence of x on y but also causality running *vice versa*, there need to be two simultaneous equations to capture the structure within the population:

$$y = \beta_0 + \beta_1 x + u \tag{8}$$

and

$$x = \gamma_0 + \gamma_1 y + v. \tag{9}$$

---

128 Waddock and Graves (1997), p. 314.

129 Waddock and Graves (1997) for instance simply run two regressions, interchanging the respective dependant variable. Though not explicitly addressing endogeneity, Luo and Bhattacharya (2006) and Roberts and Dowling (2002) chose a more sophisticated approach to account for reverse causality. Their procedure is different from that of the following study, though.

130 Cf. Börsch-Supan and Köke (2002) who also discuss other sources of endogeneity in empirical corporate governance studies.

131 Cf. Sect. 3.2 and the literature cited there.

132 Stock and Watson (2007), pp. 126–128.

133 Stock and Watson (2007), p. 189.

As can easily be shown, this leads to a covariance of x and u of

$$\mathrm{cov}(x,u) = \frac{\gamma_1 \sigma_u^2}{(1-\gamma_1\beta_1)} \neq 0.^{134} \qquad (10)$$

Since this term does not equal zero, the probability limit of the estimated coefficient $\hat{\beta}_1$ will be greater or smaller than the true coefficient β_1. In the context of this study, financial influence is said to positively affect CSP, which is why $\gamma_1 > 0$. Therefore, the simultaneous causality bias in this case leads to an overestimation of the CSP coefficients reported in Table 3.9.

The best possibility to account for simultaneous causality bias lies in random experiments. Since the data were gathered in a non-experimental setting, this possibility is not at hand. Alternatively, instrumental variable (IV) regression is a procedure that allows for consistent coefficient estimates in presence of an endogeneity problem. This technique will be subject to the following chapter.

3.3.3.4 Instrumental Variable Regression

Instrumental Variable (IV) regression is a way to consistently estimate the true coefficients of the regression function in the population in spite of endogeneity, that is when one or more of the independent variables correlate with the error term so that $\mathrm{cov}(x,u) \neq 0$. It does so by isolating the part of the variation in the endogenous variable x that correlates with the error term u from the rest of its variation (that is uncorrelated with the error term). To do this, it uses so-called instrumental variables that fulfil the characteristics of relevance and exogeneity. *Relevance* means that the instrument is correlated with the endogenous variable (to capture some of its variation), whereas *exogeneity* (often also called validity) requires that the instrument is *not* related to the error term (so that the instrument can isolate the variation in x that is exogenous). To understand the mechanism of this procedure, the following passage illustrates the procedure of IV estimation for the simple case of a linear regression with only one regressor.[135]

The population regression model relating the dependent variable y and regressor x is

$$y = \beta_0 + \beta_1 x + u, \qquad (11)$$

where $cov(x,u) \neq 0$ because of, say simultaneous causality.

Now if there is a variable z that fulfils the conditions of instrument relevance and exogeneity so that $corr(z,x) \neq 0$ and $corr(z,u) \neq 0$, it can be used to decompose the variation of x into two parts (one correlated with u and the other independent of it) by regressing x on z. This is called the reduced form equation:

$$x = \pi_0 + \pi_1 z + v. \qquad (12)$$

---

134 For the formal proof, see Stock and Watson (2007), pp. 324–325.

135 For an in-depth discussion of two-stage IV regression, cf. Greene (2003), pp. 74–80 or Wooldridge (2002), pp. 83–114.

The idea behind IV estimation is to only use the part of x which is explained by z (and hence by definition not correlated with u) and to ignore v_i (the problematic part of x). This is done in two steps. The parameters π_0, π_1 cannot be observed but can be consistently estimated by OLS on the first stage. On the second stage, the predicted (and problem-free) $\hat{x}$ are used to estimate $\hat{\beta}_o^{IV}$ as well as $\hat{\beta}_1^{IV}$ in the original equation. In the case of only one regressor, the probability limit of $\hat{\beta}_1^{IV}$ is

$$\text{plim}\,\hat{\beta}_1^{IV} = \beta_1 + \frac{\text{cov}(z,u)}{\text{cov}(z,x)}, \tag{13}$$

which is a consistent estimate if the instrument fulfils the condition of exogeneity. As can be shown formally also for the general case of one or more endogenous regressors, the IV estimates are consistent for $\boldsymbol{\beta}$ (the vector of the true regression coefficients in the population) and normally distributed in large samples.[136]

Coming back to the case of simultaneous causality between corporate social and financial performance, potential instrumental variables would have to be correlated with the respective CSP component but not with the error term, that is they should not influence *Tobin's Q* beyond their indirect effect through the CSP variables. One possibility to obtain instruments with such characteristics is to use lagged values of the endogenous variable. It is a very complex and time-consuming process to develop those competencies that are rated by sustainability rating agencies such as *oekom research* (which does not mean, however, that ratings would not change over time as the discussion in Sect. 3.4.2 will show). Since such competencies are relatively stable over time, one can assume that present CSP is influenced by past CSP, so the requirement of instrument relevance is met.[137] *oekom research* rates companies in intervals of approximately 3 years, so it is also reasonable to assume that this time difference is too long for past CSP to have an influence on financial performance. That being said, the condition of instrument exogeneity also should hold.

To check the assumption of instrumental relevance formally, one can test the null hypothesis that the partial influence of the instrument on the endogenous regressor equals zero. To perform this test, each of the instrumented variables is regressed on the instrument and all exogenous variables, respectively. Table 3.11 summarises the results of these regressions. Since all the *ceteris paribus* effects of the instruments on the respectively instrumented variables are significantly different from zero, the hypothesis of instrument *irrelevance* can be rejected. As will be discussed in the next chapter, the question is rather whether the instruments explain enough of the variance in the CSP variables to be of use for the two stage least squares (2SLS) regression.

Since u is not observable, instrument exogeneity is not testable directly. The Sargan-Test is a formal test of instrument exogeneity but only works in the case of over-identification as it requires the availability of at least one more instrument which is known to be exogenous.[138] Since in this study all reduced form equations

[136] For a proof of these properties in the general 2SLS model, cf. Wooldridge (2002), pp. 92–96.

[137] See the results in Sect. 3.2.3.

[138] Cameron and Trivedi (2005), pp. 277; Gujarati (2003), p. 713.

Table 3.11 Test of instrumental relevance

	Partial correlation of instruments and instrumented variables				
Dependent variable:	*staff*	*corpgov*	*enman*	*cust*	*soc*
Instruments					
staff (lagged)	0.1563*** (0.0800)				
corpgov (lagged)		0.3988*** (0.0000)			
enman (lagged)			0.3775*** (0.0000)		
cust (lagged)				0.3773*** (0.0000)	
soc (lagged)					0.2818*** (0.0020)
risk	−0.0278 (0.8040)	0.0845 (0.4300)	−0.1000 (0.3450)	0.0905 (0.4100)	0.1304 (0.2060)
lev	0.2972 (0.1960)	0.0072 (0.9700)	0.1079 (0.6090)	−0.0366 (0.8580)	0.1226 (0.5670)
size	0.0451 (0.2060)	−0.0416 (0.2340)	0.0798** (0.0210)	0.0689* (0.0620)	0.0365 (0.3630)
N	128	128	128	128	128
F-Value	2.7000	8.1700	9.3300	8.1300	4.9400
Prob > *F*	0.0339	0.0000	0.0000	0.0000	0.0010

OLS regression of the instrumented variables on their instruments and the exogenous variables, respectively. *p*-values ($P > t$) are reported in parentheses (calculated with heteroscedasticity-robust standard errors). Individual coefficients are statistically significant at the *10%, **5% or *** 1% level (two-tailed *t*-test). *F*-values concern the joint hypothesis that all coefficients equal zero

are exactly identified, that is there is exactly one instrument for each endogenous variable, such a formal test cannot be run here. So the instruments can only be justified on the basis of the a priori arguments outlined above.

With a valid instrument at hand, the intuitively assumed endogeneity of the CSP variables can be formally checked by means of a Hausman-Test.[139] The reasoning behind this test is as follows: since u and v in (8) and (9) are both uncorrelated with z, it follows from (9) that x_i is endogenous if and only if $cov(u,v) \neq 0$. Since v cannot be observed, one has to additionally include the residuals v of the first stage regression to the original OLS equation and test whether they are partially correlated with the regressand. To do this, one can first write the auxiliary regression[140]

$$y = \delta z + \alpha x + \rho \hat{v} + error, \tag{14}$$

[139] Wooldridge (2002), pp. 118–122.

[140] For the formal derivation, see Wooldridge (2002), p. 121 or Cameron and Trivedi (2005), pp. 275–276.

where $\hat{v}$ is the residual from the reduced form regression for x (cf. (9)). Then, one can check the null hypothesis $\rho = 0$ by means of a t-test and conclude that x is endogenous if it is rejected.

Following the procedure just described, a Hausman test was performed to formally test for endogeneity of the CSP variables. The null hypothesis of no correlation between the residuals and *Tobin's Q* could not be rejected for any of the five CSP variables, so the test failed to support the assumption of endogeneity. There is one caveat, though: since the applicability of the Hausman test heavily depends on the validity of the instruments (which cannot be tested in our case), this result does not assure that the problem of endogeneity is obsolete.[141]

After having addressed the matters of instrument relevance and exogeneity as well as the Hausman test, the 2SLS IV regression will be considered next. In the case of the model of interest here, there are five potentially endogenous dummy variables (the CSP components). Technically, the binary scaling does not pose a problem to 2SLS IV regression as both the endogenous and the instrumental variables can be binary or discrete.[142] On the first stage, the five instrumented variables require five reduced form equations, which are all exactly identified and estimated by OLS. In each equation, the CSP variable is regressed on the exogenous variables and all instruments:

$$CSP_i = \pi_0 + \boldsymbol{\pi}_{CV}\mathbf{x}_{CV} + \boldsymbol{\pi}_{IV}\mathbf{x}_{IV} + v, \tag{15}$$

where $i = 1,2,3,4,5$ indicates the five CSP component variables *staff*, *corpgov*, *enman*, *cust* and *soc*. $\mathbf{x}_{CV}$ ($\mathbf{x}_{IV}$) denotes the vector of the exogenous control variables (instrumental variables) and $\boldsymbol{\pi}_{CV}$ ($\boldsymbol{\pi}_{IV}$) the vector of the respective regression coefficients.

On the second stage, the predicted values from the first stage estimation are used instead of the original values in the regression equation:

$$Q = \beta_0 + \boldsymbol{\beta}\hat{\mathbf{x}} + u. \tag{16}$$

Again, coefficients are computed with heteroscedasticity-robust standard errors, which are also adjusted for the fact that predicted values of the endogenous variables from the first stage are used in the second stage.[143]

Because of restrictions in the sample, lagged values are only available for a subset of 128 observations. This is because certain industries included in the 2006 sample were rated for the first time so that there are no past values. In other industries, rating criteria employed by *oekom research* have changed significantly from one rating to the other so that the results are not comparable anymore. To test whether the reduction of the sample causes a selection bias, the original regression is reported together with the results of the IV estimation in Table 3.12. Columns (1) and (2) show the numbers of the one-stage OLS estimation with the full sample ($N = 294$)

[141] For detailed arguments concerning the consequences of weak instruments, cf. the discussion in the following chapter.

[142] Wooldridge (2002), p. 87.

[143] Cf. Stock and Watson (2007), p. 437.

Table 3.12 Two-stage least squares estimation results

	Instrumental variables (2SLS) regression		
Model	(1)	(2)	(3)
Regressors			
staff	−0.0379	−0.0323	−0.0747
	(0.6110)	(0.7560)	(0.9160)
corpgov	0.1780**	0.2547***	0.3550
	(0.0130)	(0.0100)	(0.2010)
enman	0.1947**	0.3323***	0.2651
	(0.0190)	(0.0050)	(0.7320)
cust	−0.1412**	−0.3297***	−0.2290
	(0.0500)	(0.0030)	(0.7200)
soc	0.1127	0.1453	−0.1830
	(0.1100)	(0.2280)	(0.7890)
risk	−0.1060	0.0249	0.0625
	(0.2590)	(0.8490)	(0.7860)
lev	−1.8294***	−2.1060***	−2.0444***
	(0.0000)	(0.0000)	(0.0000)
size	−0.1096***	−0.1313***	−0.1028**
	(0.0000)	(0.0000)	(0.0200)
Constant	1.6086***	1.5550***	1.6976***
	(0.0000)	(0.0000)	(0.0000)
N	294	128	128
Prob > *F*	0.0000	0.0000	0.0000
R^2	0.4431	0.5315	0.4811
F(CSP)	3.86***	4.13***	0.75

Dependent variable: *Tobin's Q*. *p*-values ($P > t$) are reported in parentheses (calculated with heteroscedasticity-robust standard errors). Individual coefficients are statistically significant at the *10%, **5% or ***1% level (two-tailed *t*-test). Model 1 reports the original OLS estimation with the full sample, model 2 shows the results for the reduced sample. Model 3 reports the 2SLS estimates. Regressors *staff*, *corpgov*, *enman*, *cust* and *soc* are instrumented. Instruments: *staff (lagged)*, *corpgov (lagged)*, *enman (lagged)*, *cust (lagged)*, *soc (lagged)*, *risk*, *lev*, *size*. F(CSP) gives the F-statistic to test the joint hypothesis that all CSP variables equal zero

and the reduced sample ($N = 128$), respectively. Column (3) reports the coefficients from the second stage of the instrumental variable regression. As one can see, the results do not change very much after reducing the sample: the directions do not alter and the coefficients remain significant. With the IV regression, however, the coefficient estimates of the single CSP component become very imprecise due to the large standard errors. In none of the five cases can the null hypothesis be rejected that the coefficients equal zero.

3.3.3.5 Limitations to IV Regression Analysis

The preceding discussion intended to qualify the results of the previous analyses in the light of the problem of endogeneity. This being done, the question is what can be followed from this analysis and, arguably even more important, what can *not* be followed from it.

The answer to that question eventually depends on the assumed quality of the instruments. If the instruments in use were valid and relevant, one could argue that the results of the former estimation need to be revised, because after accounting for endogeneity no relation between *Tobin's Q* and any of the CSP variables can be shown statistically.

However, the fact that the analysis did not yield consistent estimates after accounting for endogeneity does not render all results obsolete. The correlations in the sample that were revealed by the cross-sectional OLS analysis still exist. They just do not allow for inference of the kind that a change in certain CSP variables would causally determine a change in *Tobin's Q*.

The interpretation of the results becomes a bit more complicated if one considers the quality of the instruments to be problematic. Specifically, three problems arise in the context of this study what regards the IV regression employed. All of them root in the problem that instruments might be weakly correlated with the variables being instrumented.

First, because of the availability of *oekom* data, the sample with observations for two different points in time is not very large. Such small samples can lead to biased estimates and standard errors, especially when instruments are weak.[144] *Second*, even in very large samples, the IV estimator can be problematic if the instruments are weak. As one can easily see from (13), the probability limit of the estimate is different from the true coefficient if the instrument is not exogenous. This difference becomes even bigger in the case of weak instruments: if there is only a very small correlation between the instrument z and the endogenous variable x, the estimator becomes very large.

A *third* problem of IV regression is that the standard errors of the estimates typically become very large. Stated formally, the asymptotic variance of the coefficient in the case of only one regressor is

$$\text{Avar}(\hat{\beta}_1^{IV}) = \frac{\text{Avar}(\hat{\beta}_1^{OLS})}{r_{xz}^2}, \tag{17}$$

where r_{xz}^2 is the sample correlation between x and z.[145] This illustrates that the variance of the IV estimator is necessarily larger than that of OLS (unless the very unlikely case of corr $(x, z) = 1$) and that a weak correlation between x and z exacerbates this problem.

There is no definite way to test for weakness of instruments. But to begin with, the hypothesis of irrelevant instruments was rejected on the basis of their partial correlation with the endogenous variables (cf. Table 3.11). Additionally, as a rule of thumb it is often suggested that the F-statistic on the first stage should be higher

144 See Cameron and Trivedi (2005), pp. 108–109, for a discussion of such a 'finite sample bias'. As Wooldridge (2002), p. 101, mentions, expected values do not even have an expected value in small samples.

145 Cameron and Trivedi (2005), p. 107.

than 10 and by no means lower than 5.[146] According to this rule, especially the instruments for the variables *staff* and *soc* would be problematic.

Although the coefficients did not become very large (which would have been predicted for small samples and weak instruments), the estimates had very large standard errors, which lead to the problem that the coefficients all became non-significant.

3.3.4 Conclusions

The aim of Chap. 3 was the empirical analysis of the CSP/CFP-link within the differentiated framework developed before. As a consequence of these various analyses, several conclusions can be drawn up to this point while other questions still need to be addressed in the following. In contrast to previous claims and empirical work, the null hypothesis of no relation between *Tobin's Q* (or return on equity) and an over-all CSP measure could not be rejected. This result can be interpreted as the empirical confirmation of the conceptually derived argument that (desirable as it might be) it is not reasonable to assume a positive generic link between CSR and private profits. However, single components of CSR did show to be related to firm success. Within a more differentiated framework, positive correlations between *Tobin's Q* and a good performance within the components of *Corporate Governance and Business Ethics* as well as *Environmental Management and Eco-Efficiency* were found. In the case of environmental performance, this link did not exist unconditionally, though its positive association with *Tobin's Q* proved to be higher for those firms that belong to heavy polluting industries.

Surprisingly, *Customer and Product Responsibility* is negatively correlated with *Tobin's Q*. However, this relation disappeared after changes in the measure of financial performance. Beyond this, there was no evidence for a negative association between social and financial performance. Taken together, the reported results can be assumed to be substantial as they were mainly robust towards changes in the financial performance measure and towards a reduction of the sample size by more than half.

In spite of these results, the question of 'slack resources' vs. 'good management' remains open. This possibly simultaneous causality of financial and social performance lends support to the argument that the estimated coefficients are not consistent due to problems of endogeneity. In an attempt to control for endogeneity, the IV estimator failed to confirm the previous results, which can on the one hand be used to question the validity of the previous results. On the other hand, since the instruments risk being weak, the large standard errors (and therefore insignificant coefficients) are not surprising. In the end, there is no definite way to decide

---

146 This argument goes back to Staiger and Stock (1997) and Stock and Yogo (2005) who show that a first-stage F-statistic higher than 10 (5) corresponds to an estimator bias of less than 10% (20%). See also Cameron and Trivedi (2005), pp. 108–109 and Stock and Watson (2007), p. 466.

whether the possibly inconsistent OLS estimators or the consistent but imprecise 2SLS results are more reliable.[147]

Eventually, it is safe to conclude that the correlations revealed in the OLS analysis persist irrespective of causality. Moreover, it should be stressed that the failure to prove negative correlations is an important result as well. Apparently, above-average expenditures for CSR causes do not necessarily lead to financial underperformance. This at least stands in contrast to the neoclassical arguments according to which CSR is a waste of resources.[148]

3.4 An Analysis of Changes in CSP and CFP

3.4.1 Motivation and Method of Analysis

A common problem with cross-sectional regression analysis is the omitted variables bias.[149] If the population model contains explanatory variables that the estimated model fails to include because they are unobservable, OLS risks producing inconsistent estimates. Applied to the context of this study, firm financial performance could for instance be influenced by certain firm characteristics that are relatively constant over time and that are correlated with the CSP or the control variables (consider firm culture or management ability as an example). If such effects exist and if no data are available to measure them, inconsistent estimates due to the omitted variables problem are likely.[150]

One commonly applied solution to this problem is the use of panel data and respective econometric methods that produce consistent coefficient estimates in presence of omitted variables that do not change over time.[151] In panel data sets, each entity (i.e. in our case the company) is observed at more than one time periods. Although *oekom research* has been rating companies since 1994, their data cannot be used to construct a panel data set throughout their entire history due to technical restrictions. First, in the course of time, companies dropped out of the ratings while others were added later. Second, some rating criteria of certain industries changed through the years so that these ratings of different points in time are incomparable. However, there is a sub-sample of the data employed in the cross-sectional analysis

[147] Cf. Wooldridge (2002), p. 104.

[148] Cf. the earlier discussion in Sect. "The Neoclassical Approach Vs. The Business Case Hypothesis".

[149] Cf. Gujarati (2003), pp. 517–524. Wooldridge (2002), pp. 61–63.

[150] It should be noted that this omitted variable problem only leads to endogeneity if the left out variable is correlated with one of the regressors. See also Wooldridge (2002), p. 247.

[151] Cf. Stock and Watson (2007), p. 318. A very common approach to analysing the effects of changes in the independent variable are event studies, cf. McWilliams and Siegel (1997). However, *oekom* data are not publicly available and are not published simultaneously for all industries. Therefore, it is not plausible to assume any observable effect of the industry ratings on financial markets, so that this method cannot be applied here.

(from 2006), for which earlier ratings are available.[152] This sub-sample only contains companies that are also included in the 2006 data set and that were rated according to the same criteria so that the grades are fully comparable.[153] Technically, panel data analyses only require a minimum of two time periods, so that such methods can be performed with these data.

To illustrate how panel data can eliminate unobserved time-constant effects, consider the following equation for the unobserved effects model[154]:

$$y_{it} = \mathbf{x}_{it}\boldsymbol{\beta} + c_i + u_{it}, \tag{18}$$

where y_{it} is the regressand, vector $\mathbf{x}_{it}$ contains the constant (=1) and the explanatory variables, vector $\boldsymbol{\beta}$ contains the regression coefficients (including the constant coefficient) and u_{it} the error term. $i = 1, \ldots n$ indexes the observational units (entities) and $t = 1, 2$ is the time period index. The variable c represents an unobserved, time-constant effect that influences the regressand.

Two different estimation methods are commonly used to analyse panel data. Depending on the correctness of the assumption, both methods yield consistent results in spite of unobserved effects. These are the random effect estimation and the fixed effects estimation. The random effects (RE) approach to estimating $\boldsymbol{\beta}$ includes c_i into the composite error $v_{it} = c_i + u_{it}$ and then accounts for the implied serial correlation by using a so-called feasible generalised least squares (FGLS) analysis. In contrast, the fixed effects (FE) estimator accounts for c_i by transforming the data over time and then pooling all data into one OLS regression. Both methods require strict exogeneity of the regressors to produce consistent estimates, that is no element of $\mathbf{x}_t$ must be correlated with the error terms in any period so that $\operatorname{cov}(\mathbf{x}_t, u_s) = \mathbf{0}$ for all $t = 1, \ldots, T$ and $s = 1, \ldots, T$. But the two methods differ in their conception of the relation between the unobserved and the observed variables. RE estimation requires that $\operatorname{cov}(\mathbf{x}_t, c) = \mathbf{0}$, whereas FE allows for such a correlation. Thus, whether FE or RE estimation is the appropriate estimation method essentially boils down to the question of whether or not c_i is orthogonal to $\mathbf{x}_{it}$.[155]

If there are any relevant unobserved firm characteristics in the context of this study, these are most likely to be correlated with the CSP variables. Management capability, firm culture or its ability to innovate could all influence *Tobin's Q* and at the same time the CSP variables. Thus, FE estimation is the appropriate estimation method in this context.

---

152 These data for past CSP were also used during the probit analyses in Sect. 3.2 as well as for the IV estimation in Sect. 3.3.3.4. These ratings were conducted in the years 2002 and 2003. As with the later ratings, these can be assumed to be relatively stable over 1 year so that all ratings are take for CSP measures of the year 2003.

153 Actually there were some differences in the constructions of the *crr*, *scr* and *er* grades. However, these differences did not concern the single items, so that – compared to 2006 – a structurally identical rating could be reconstructed on the basis of the 2003 data.

154 The following discussion is based on Wooldridge (2002), pp. 247–291, where the term 'unobserved effects model' is derived from.

155 Considering the FE vs. RE decision, see also Gujarati (2003), pp. 650–651. Another question is whether $\mathbf{x}_{it}$ includes time-invariant elements. This is not possible with RE estimation, which requires variation in all elements of $\mathbf{x}_{it}$.

Table 3.13 Descriptive statistics for differenced variables

Variable	Obs	Mean	Std. Dev.	min	max	% ↓	% –	% ↑
Δcrr	128	0.0313	0.5461	−1	1	13.28	70.31	16.41
$\Delta staff$	128	0.0547	0.6437	−1	1	17.97	58.59	23.44
$\Delta corpgov$	128	−0.0547	0.5370	−1	1	17.19	71.09	11.72
$\Delta enman$	128	0.0313	0.5603	−1	1	14.06	68.75	17.19
$\Delta cust$	128	0.0391	0.5528	−1	1	13.28	69.53	17.19
Δsoc	128	0.1094	0.5783	−1	1	11.72	65.63	22.66
$\Delta Tobin$	128	0.1068	0.4323	−2.0452	1.5764			
$\Delta risk$	128	−0.0423	0.4464	−1.1505	1.3650			
Δlev	128	−0.0146	0.0690	−0.2909	0.2573			
$\Delta size$	128	0.3203	0.3332	−0.9639	1.4926			

Table reports differences in the respectives variables from 2006 to 2003 (e.g. $\Delta Tobin = Tobin_{2006} - Tobin_{2003}$). % ↓, % – and % ↑ give the percantage of companies that have improved, worsened or stayed equal in their CSR performance (formerly binary variables now take values −1, 0, 1, respectively)

The idea behind FE estimation is that it estimates one intercept for each entity. In the special case of only two points in time, the time-constant unobservable c_i can be eliminated by differencing (18) for the two time periods. This yields $\Delta y_i = \Delta \mathbf{x}_i \boldsymbol{\beta} + \Delta u_i$ (where Δ indicates differences in time, i.e. $\Delta y = y_2 - y_1$ etc.), which equals a 'differenced' standard linear model without the constant. In addition, including an intercept allows for effects that vary across time but not across the observations (e.g. the macro-economic situation).[156] This equation can thus consistently be estimated by OLS in spite of the presence of unobservable effects and yields exactly the same results as FE estimation. To obtain consistent estimates even in the case of serial correlation, the condition of strict exogeneity has to hold, however.[157] This requires that no element of $\mathbf{x}_t$ is correlated with the error terms in both periods so that $\text{cov}(\mathbf{x}_t, u_s)=\mathbf{0}$ for all $t = 1, 2$ and $s = 1, 2$.

The following section will present the results of the FE model. Before that, Table 3.13 provides descriptive statistics for the differenced variables to provide an overview on how the measures have changed from the earlier rating to that of 2006.

3.4.2 Test Results for the Analysis of Changes in CSP and CFP

As the previous analysis in the context of the IV regression revealed, the results of the cross-sectional OLS estimation were robust to a reduction of the sample to

[156] Cf. Greene (2003), p. 291.

[157] If this condition holds and if $\text{cov}(\mathbf{x}_t, c) = \mathbf{0}$, pooled OLS also yields unbiased and consistent estimates. However, an additionally third condition has to hold which rules out serial correlation of the error terms: $E(u_t u_s | \mathbf{x}_t \mathbf{x}_s) = 0$, $t \neq s$, $t, s = 1, \ldots T$. See Wooldridge (2002), pp. 169–179 and pp. 248–249. In the case of $T = 2$, there are three possibilities that yield identical regression coefficient estimates. The regression model with first differences, as described above; FE regression (within-distance) with a dummy for the time period; and pooled OLS including one dummy for each observation.

Table 3.14 Results of the fixed effects OLS model (within transformation)

FE Regression Results			
Regressors	(1)	(2)	(3)
crr	0.0184 (0.0704)		
staff		0.0862 (0.0665)	0.0920 (0.0885)
corpgov		−0.0360 (0.0740)	−0.0110 (0.0880)
enman		−0.0392 (0.0743)	0.0064 (0.1171)
cust		−0.0460 (0.0773)	−0.0370 (0.0802)
soc		0.0766 (0.0681)	0.0683 (0.0718)
risk	0.2059** (0.0915)	0.2134** (0.0924)	0.2245** (0.0952)
lev	−0.3472 (0.5513)	−0.3145 (0.5541)	−0.3426 (0.5671)
size	0.0738 (0.1210)	0.0995 (0.1236)	0.0894 (0.1307)
enman × *class*			−0.0413 (0.1415)
enman × *size*			−0.0056 (0.0111)
staff × *size*			−0.0003 (0.0121)
corpgov × *size*			−0.0051 (0.0102)
year06	0.0862 (0.0558)	0.0673 (0.0571)	0.0206 (0.0913)
Const	0.7436 (1.2069)	0.4515 (1.2307)	1.3107 (0.8390)
N_{obs}	256	256	256
N_{groups}	128	128	128
Prob > *F*	0.0098***	0.0327**	0.1352

Dependent variable: *Tobin's Q*. *p*-values ($P > t$) are reported in parentheses. Individual coefficients are statistically significant at the *10%, **5% or ***1% level (two-tailed *t*-test). The dummy variable *year06* measures time fixed effects between the two points in time of measurement (2003 and 2006)

those observations that are available for two points in time.[158] Thus, if the FE model yields different results, these cannot merely be explained by changes in the sample due to its reduction.

Table 3.14 reports the results of the fixed effects regression (calculated by a within transformation). As before, column (1) refers to the model which includes the over-all *crr* grade as the only CSP variable. Its coefficient is positive but

[158] Cf. column (2) in Table 3.12.

far away from any satisfying significance level. In stark contrast to the previous cross-sectional OLS analysis, *lev* and *size* are not significantly different from zero, whereas *risk* is the only variable with a positive coefficient which significantly differs from zero. That is, those companies that increased in risk from one period to the other also displayed a *Tobin's Q*, which was higher than that of the previous period. Column (2) which includes all five stakeholder-related differenced CSP variables is qualitatively identical to the first model. None of these variables proves to have a significant influence on *Tobin's Q*. The same applies to column (3), which reports the estimates for the model including all interaction effects. Although the individual coefficients are comparable with columns (2) and (3), the entire model fails to be significant.

Taken together, the FE models do not confirm any of the previously obtained results. The following chapter will discuss conclusions that can be drawn from this outcome.

3.4.3 Significance of the Results

The hypothesis that all coefficients equal zero is rejected on the 1% and the 5% level in models (1) and (2), respectively. Also, the regression results qualitatively do not change if computed with RE estimation. The significance of the results can thus not be denied on the basis of the models altogether. On first sight, it therefore seems that none of the results of the prior analysis can be maintained once time constant firm characteristics are included in a panel analysis by fixed effects regression. However, a number of technical problems is involved with panel data analysis and is thus relevant to the interpretation of its results.

As the descriptive statistics showed, there is only relatively little variation in the CSP variables. In four of the five CSP components, more than two-thirds of the companies remained within the same (low or high) performance class across both time periods (the exception is *staff* where this applies to 59% of the sample). The fact that there are only so few changes surely puts certain limitations to the results' robustness and reliability. Another shortcoming lies in the fact that there are only 128 observations for which data are available for two time periods ($T = 2$). Although technically two time periods are enough to perform these estimations, FE estimation requires a large number of observations (N) to justify asymptotic results such as consistent estimates of β.

As explained earlier, FE (as well as RE) estimation requires the assumption of strict exogeneity (i.e. no element of the covariate vector $\mathbf{x}_{it}$ is correlated with the error term in any time period). Considering the problem of endogeneity discussed in Sect. 3.3.3, this assumption might be violated. The problem here is that the fixed effects estimator of $\boldsymbol{\beta}$ is inconsistent when strict exogeneity does not hold. Moreover, the size of the inconsistency depends on T: if $T = 2$, as in our case, the violation of strict exogeneity can lead to estimates that are wrong in size and even in sign.[159]

Motivated by these problems, alternative methods have been developed that produce consistent estimates even if the assumption of strict exogeneity is violated. A very popular and often employed method in this context is the Arellano–Bond estimator.[160] The general idea of it is to eliminate unobserved effects using a within transformation (or differencing) and then to use lagged values of all model variables as instruments in a generalised methods of moments (GMM) approach.[161] Since this estimator requires differenced equations *and* lagged values, it is not applicable for this study, where data are only available for two points in time.

In light of these technical problems, the results of the preceding cannot be considered as very robust and significant. In sum, the analysis of two time observations has failed to either confirm or reject the previous results on the CSP/CFP link.

3.5 Testing the Hypothesis of Decreasing Marginal Effects of CSP

3.5.1 The Hypothesis of Decreasing Marginal Effects of CSR Investments

An argument commonly found in conceptual and theoretical works on CSR is that even if it might be plausible to assume a business case for CSR, this assumption holds true only to a limited extent.[162] This argument becomes clear if one conceives of CSP as a continuum between worst-possible and best-possible CSP and considers the development of the costs and benefits of an incremental improvement of CSP along this continuum. Marginal costs of CSP improvements can be assumed not to be constant all along but to increase with the level of CSP as it becomes more and more difficult to further enhance CSP if a company already performs at a high level. Marginal benefits, however, decrease with higher CSP since the internal and external effects described earlier are most relevant as long as the opportunities associated with CSP are not exploited, yet. To consider some of the examples mentioned earlier, consumers do not pay premium prices for environmentally friendly products to an unlimited extent; employee motivation will not infinitely increase because of a higher identification with their company; capital costs due to lower risk will not fall to zero because of a good CSR reputation, etc. Consequently, there is a level of CSP

[159] For numerical illustrations of how large inconsistencies can become with small values of T, cf. Hsiao (2003), p. 361.

[160] Arellano and Bond (1991); for a treatment of unobserved effects models without the assumption of strict exogeneity, cf. Wooldridge (2002), pp. 299–315.

[161] Greene (2003), pp. 307–314; Wooldridge (2002), p. 304.

[162] Smith (2003), p. 70; Ullman (1985), p. 542; and, in the context of SRI funds, Barnett and Salomon (2006).

at which the marginal benefits of additional investments into CSP equal its marginal costs. When corporate expenditures for CSR exceed this threshold, the marginal net effects of these investments turn negative so that the net gain π of CSP falls below its optimum π^*.

To illustrate these relations, the net gain π of improvements in CSP can be depicted as a concave function of CSP. Its slope continually decreases until it finally turns negative. As shown in Fig. 3.7, the point at which $\frac{\delta\pi}{\delta CSP} = 0$ (where marginal costs equal marginal benefits) defines the optimal level of CSP from the firm perspective, yielding maximum net gains.[163]

Given such a relation between the level of CSP and its net gains, the Friedman-like anti-CSR arguments turn into the question up to which point exactly CSR investments are rational in an economic sense. This question can, on the one hand, be addressed theoretically by analysing the costs and benefits of CSP in a specific setting and thereby determining the optimal level of CSR.[164] On the other hand, one can also empirically ask whether companies that reach an exceptionally high CSR

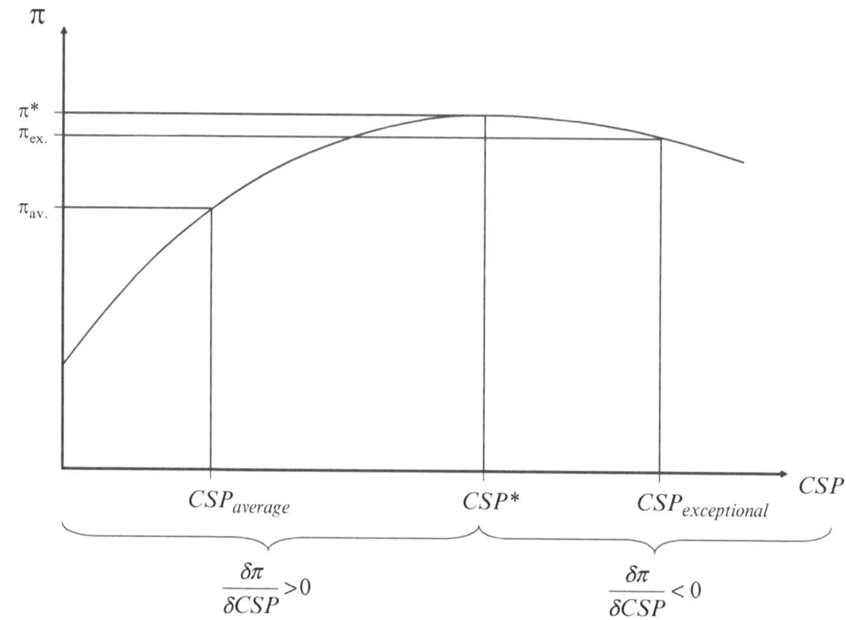

Fig. 3.7 Decreasing marginal effects of continuous CSP investments

[163] For comparable visualisations of the inversed U-shaped curve, cf. Bowman (1973), p. 25; Picot (1977), p. 33; Schaltegger and Synnestvedt (2002), p. 341; Wagner (2002), p. 135; Wagner and Schaltegger (2004), p. 558.

[164] McWilliams and Siegel (2001) claim that such a point exists. However, they do not formally show how it can exactly be determined. For a mathematical formalisation of this idea, see Baron (2005).

ranking have to bear costs that are higher than the benefits, and therefore financially perform worse than those companies that just have a rating beyond average.

Such questions have seldom been explicitly addressed in the empirical CSR literature. In an early study, Bowman and Haire (1975) form three classes on the basis of different CSP measures and ask whether there are group mean differences in the groups' financial performance measured by return on equity (ROE). They find significant differences: the medium group has the highest ROE but the group with the best CSP rating had an average ROE higher than that of the worst group, but still lower than the medium group. Consequently, they interpret their results as a support for the assumption of an inverted U-shaped curve relation between profits and CSP. These results are problematic for methodological reasons, though. Apart from difficulties concerning the CSP measure[165] no *ceteris paribus* analysis was conducted so that it remains unclear what other kinds of differences persisted in the three groups that were not controlled for.

In a different approach, Barnett and Salomon (2006) analyse the performance of SRI funds and consider the variance within these funds' screening strategies. They find that the funds with the strictest as well as those with the loosest screening criteria perform best and that those 'stuck in the middle' under-perform on the market. In contrast to the Bowman and Haire (1975) study, this corresponds to a U-shaped relationship between CSP and profits. However, given the very different approaches and measurement strategies, these two studies are difficult to compare.

3.5.2 Empirical Test

The hypothesis of decreasing (and eventually negative) marginal effects of CSP can also be empirically tested with the data employed in this study. However, the categorical scaling of the CSP variables does not allow for a direct test of the curvilinear relation discussed earlier. Alternatively, it translates into the question whether the positive relation between certain CSP variables and *Tobin's Q* changes as soon as we distinguish three instead of two groups per variable (rather than a continuum): a first group that consists of companies with ratings below the industry mean (*low performers*); a second with ratings higher than the mean but lower than the 75 percentile (*good performers*); and a third group that includes the top 25% performers of a given industry (*excellent performers*).[166] Since only two of the CSP variables proved to show a positive relation with *Tobin's Q* in the preceding analysis, tests can only meaningfully be run for these two variables.

The following hypotheses, which can be tested by means of *oekom* data, capture the ideas discussed up to this point:

---

[165] Cf. the discussion of their methodological approach on page 22.

[166] A cut at the 0.9 percentile would have been more desirable to identify the real top performers. However, because of some industries with comparably few companies, this procedure would have resulted in too few observations in the best performance class.

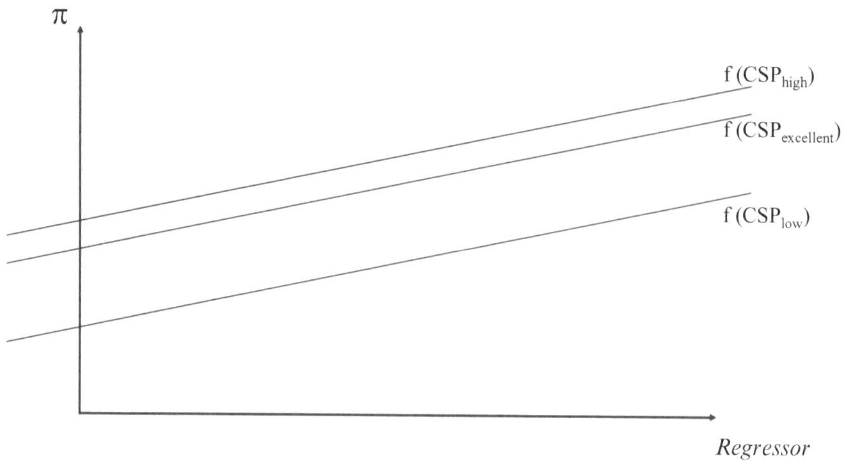

Fig. 3.8 Comparing the effects of CSP with binary variables

H_{3a}: Good performers along the CSP components *corpgov* and *enman*, will c.p. display a higher *Tobin's Q* than low performers.

H_{3b}: Excellent performers along these components will c.p. display a lower *Tobin's Q* than good performers, but still higher than that of low performers.

To be able to construct the differences between low, good and excellent performers, three groups have been constructed that are captured by two binary variables for each of these two dimensions. $corpgov_{good}(enman_{good})$ takes value 1 if the company performs beyond the respective industry mean but still below the 75% quantile, and 0 otherwise. $corpgov_{excellent}(enman_{excellent})$ takes value 1 if the company performs among the respective industry's top 25% class, and 0 otherwise.

Binary variables employed in OLS regressions indicate the *ceteris paribus* effect on the average difference in the dependent variable between the groups that take value 0 and 1 on the dummy variable, respectively. The hypothesis to be tested then is whether excellent performers regarding *corpgov* and *enman ceteris paribus* have a different mean in *Tobin's Q*.

Formally, the equation to be estimated is

$$Q = \beta_0 + \beta_1 corpgov_{good} + \beta_2 corpgov_{exc} + \beta_3 enman_{good} + \beta_4 enman_{exc} + \\ + \beta_5 staff + \beta_6 soc + \beta_7 cust + \beta_8 risk + \beta_9 lev + \beta_{10} size + u. \tag{19}$$

In terms of (19), H_{3a} and H_{3b} translate into the expectation that $\beta_1 > \beta_2 > 0$ and that $\beta_3 > \beta_4 > 0$. Graphically, the estimated coefficient of a dummy variable in a regression analysis represents the size of a shift of the intercept if the dummy takes value 1. In the case of only one regressor, this can be visualised as in Fig. 3.8.[167]

[167] Since the model actually tested has more than one continuous regressor, it cannot be visualised in such a graph.

To test whether the insignificant results of the over-all CSP variable *crr* changes when groups are more differentiated then just good/bad performers, *crr* was included for the three groups in a separate analysis analogously to the other two CSP variables.

3.5.3 Test Results and Discussion

Table 3.15 reports the results of the OLS estimation. Column (1) contains the model with two more differentiated *crr* variables and column (3) shows the estimates for (19). For better comparability, column (2) repeats the results from the original estimation discussed in Sect. 3.3.2.

As column (1) shows, *crr* does not have a significant influence on *Tobin's Q*. That is consistent with all results obtained so far and is one more indicator for the lacking adequateness of considering CSP at such an aggregated level. Concerning those variables in column (3) that have also been included in column (2), the results remain nearly unaltered with respect to sign and size.

The coefficient estimates of the different performance-groups do not support hypothesis H_{3b}. Although, as predicted by H_{3a}, good performers ($gorpgov_{good}$, $nman_{good}$) still display a higher *Tobin's Q* than their low-performing counterparts, the coefficient of $gorpgov_{excellent}(enman_{excellent})$ is numerically higher than that of $gorpgov_{good}(enman_{good})$. However, a Wald test failed to defeat the linear hypotheses that the coefficients are identical ($\beta_1 = \beta_2$ and $\beta_3 = \beta_4$) so that there is no reason to assume any financial performance differences between the good and the excellent groups with respect to *gorpgov* and *enman*. Hence, the results of the analysis run counter to the hypothesis that the best performers have to bear costs that outweigh the benefits of their superior performance. That is, although there is a significant difference in *Tobin's Q* between good and low performers what concerns *Corporate Governance and Business Ethics* (the difference with regards to *Environmental Management and Eco-Efficiency* is also positive but not significant), there is no significant difference between good and excellent performers.

These results can be interpreted in several ways. On the one hand, they could be used to challenge the validity of the hypothesis of decreasing marginal effects of CSP. One could argue that the hypothesis is simply wrong as there is no one-directional causal effect anyway. Even though there might be a correlation between firm success and single measures of CSP, no clear causal direction exists within this relation. Therefore, exceptional CSP logically cannot be associated with inferior financial performance. From that perspective, even the opposite is the case: the most successful companies have the most resources available for CSR expenditures. And even if such investments become too high to be justified by their positive economic effects, they are too small to have an impact on a measure as abstract as *Tobin's Q*.

Alternatively, the results obtained can be explained without rejecting the assumption of decreasing marginal effects. One could argue that although this hypothesis is theoretically appealing, it cannot be verified empirically with the data set at hand.

Table 3.15 Test results for low, good and excellent performers

Regressors	(1)	(2)	(3)
	Regression for testing decreasing marginal effects (OLS estimation)		
crr_{good}	−0.0135		
	(0.8820)		
$crr_{excellent}$	0.0651		
	(0.4160)		
staff		−0.0379	−0.0338
		(0.6110)	(0.6560)
corpgov		0.1780**	
		(0.0130)	
$corpgov_{good}$			0.1645*
			(0.0980)
$corpgov_{excellent}$			0.1785**
			(0.0400)
enman		0.1947**	
		(0.0190)	
$enman_{good}$			0.1334
			(0.1640)
$enman_{excellent}$			0.2284**
			(0.0180)
cust		−0.1412**	−0.1465**
		(0.0500)	(0.0340)
soc		0.1127	0.1043
		(0.1970)	(0.2350)
risk	−0.0594	−0.1060	−0.1070
	(0.5240)	(0.2590)	(0.2540)
lev	−1.8103***	−1.8294***	−1.8496***
	(0.0000)	(0.0000)	(0.0000)
size	−0.1091***	−0.1096***	−0.1104***
	(0.0000)	(0.0000)	(0.0000)
Constant	1.6320***	1.4938***	1.5193***
	(0.0000)	(0.0000)	(0.0000)
N	294	294	294
Prob > *F*	0.0000	0.0000	0.0000
R^2	0.4101	0.4431	0.4430

Dependent variable: *Tobin's Q*. Heteroscedasticity-robust standard errors are reported in parentheses. Individual coefficients are statistically significant at the *10%, **5% or ***1% level (two-tailed *t*-test). 'Good' performers along *crr*, *corpgov* and *enman* perform higher than the respective industry mean but lower than the 0.75 quantile; 'excellent' perform higher than 'good'

Some of the companies in the sample might fall below the optimal level of CSP and therefore forfeit an opportunity to maximise profits. However, none of them has moved beyond that threshold. Since the classes were formed in relation to the respective industry, the variables are not an absolute but a relative social performance measure, so even the 'excellent' performers have not reached a level of CSP, which would go beyond economic reasoning. Thus, although excellent CSP *would* lead to lower financial performance in the case of over-investments, such cases are not observable within the sample used in the study.

In any case, the data failed to lend support to the argument that 'too high' investments in CSR are statistically associated with lower financial performance.[168] Although there still is a positive relation between *corpgov* and *enman* on the one side and *Tobin's Q* on the other, this relation is not significantly qualified by further distinguishing low, good and excellent performers along these CSP variables.

[168] A regression with return on equity (ROE) as the dependent variable was also conducted but did not yield qualitatively different results.

Chapter 4
Conclusions Concerning Empirical Evidence for the Business Case for Corporate Social Responsibility

4.1 Conclusions and Limitations to the Study

The purpose of this research was to analyse the underlying logic of and empirical evidence for the business case for corporate social responsibility. To do this, it critically examined conceptual and empirical literature on CSR in general and on the CSP/CFP-link in particular. Additionally, it performed an empirical study with data from the German CSR rating company *oekom research* to test conceptually derived hypotheses and to gain insights into the empirical relation between corporate social and financial performance.

The conceptual investigation developed a generic framework for the analysis of such relations. After reviewing philosophical concepts of responsibility, it defined CSR as a multi-relational and multi-dimensional construct, which refers to ascriptions of responsibilities in response to perceived moral conflicts. It was argued that these ascriptions can best be classified according to the stakeholder approach, which allows for a differentiated analysis of corporate reactions to ascribed responsibilities and their consequences. Moreover, the analysis stressed the need to exactly scrutinise distinct mechanisms to better understand why and under what circumstances it might be reasonable to assume a business case for CSR.

As was shown in the empirical analysis of the most relevant drivers of CSP, company size and past social performance turned out to be two important determinants. Concerning the environmental rating, past performance proved to be especially important in predicting actual performance. The fact that this relation was not that strong in the case of the social-cultural component of the rating suggests that it is much easier to improve on that dimension than it is with regards to environmental performance. In contrast to what was expected, neither past financial performance nor the regional background of the company helped explain differences in responsibility ratings. Another result was that companies performing well along one stakeholder-related dimension are also very likely to perform high on the others. This suggests that most of the companies pursue coherent CSR strategies, and either try to perform well on many CSP components or display minor performance on most criteria simultaneously.

P. Schreck, *The Business Case for Corporate Social Responsibility*,
Contributions to Management Science.

The subsequent empirical analysis of the link between corporate social and financial performance failed to deliver a clear and unambiguous picture as to the empirical business case for CSR. These outcomes generally suggest that – though frequently claimed – there is no empirical basis for the assumption of a generic CSP/CFP-link. At first, the cross-sectional regression analysis showed some interesting results as to the relationship between certain CSP components and *Tobin's Q*, which confirmed parts of the hypotheses. The most important results were robust to changes in measures of financial performance. However, the analysis failed to support the assumption of a *causal* CSP/CFP-link, as revealed by the instrumental variable regression. It remains unclear, though, whether this result is due to the poor quality (weak relevance) of the instruments or due to endogeneity. After all, neither the Hausman test nor the results of Sect. 3.2 indicate that past financial performance predicts CSP. Finally, the panel data analysis did not yield any direct results. Although this was partly ascribed to technical difficulties, the analysis failed to confirm any of the previously obtained effects. In the light of these sobering results, it is only safe to say that financially successful companies tend to display superior performance on certain CSP dimensions (*enman* and *corpgov*), regardless of a causal link. This conclusion is in line with the aforementioned 'good management' argument. Apparently, the management of successful companies also sees it as a necessity to display good environmental performance and to subscribe to principles of good corporate governance.

In those cases where there was a link between CFP and CSP, no support was found for the hypothesis of decreasing marginal effects. The excellent performers along the dimensions *enman* and *corpgov* had an average *Tobin's Q*, which did not significantly differ from that of their lower (but still well) performing counterparts.

Considering the nature of CSR and its link to financial performance, these ambiguous results are rather expectable, and all too clear results would have been very surprising. The outcomes of the empirical analysis revealed how complex CSR matters and their internal as well as external effects are once one leaves the conceptual level and scrutinises actual performances. If the empirical relations were that clear, there would be no basis for the controversial debates on CSR. This is exactly why it is so interesting to ask in which cases private and public profits do not fall apart. After all, there would be no need to convince companies to implement CSR strategies if that automatically leads to additional profits. If that were the case, corporate violations of societal norms and values would be very unlikely, and companies would differ very little in their performances as to CSR (which is clearly not the case). This leads to another important conclusion: the empirical evidence does not lend support to a purely instrumental view on CSR. In the light of the results of this study, CSR investments cannot solely be justified with reference to their economically sound effects. In this context, it is an evenly important result of the preceding analysis that efforts to align corporate decisions and actions with moral standards do not come along with financial penalties, either.

The study is of course subject to certain limitations. The analysis is restricted to the data made available by *oekom research*. On the one hand, this is a limited dataset as it comprises only selected companies, which regards firm size as well as industries, and as it does not provide comprehensive panel data. On the other hand, arguments were brought forward suggesting that these data are more suitable for the research aim than those used in earlier studies. Additionally, the study has treated companies as 'black boxes' and thus forms a very generic analysis. Firm success has been operationalised by the highly abstract measure of *Tobin's Q* and has been analysed across numerous companies. Although this is a very common procedure in the finance literature, the use of such measures leaves out many specific individual firm aspects that concern performance at the specific year of analysis.[1] Another limitation due to technical reasons was the lacking in-depth investigation of contingencies that determine under which circumstances a business case for CSR can exist. Such analyses would have required a lot more observations for each industry so that more precise industry-specific effects could have been taken into account. Moreover, this study's research methodology is not designed to provide insights into actual, real-world decision processes concerning CSR investments. The question whether explicit CSR strategies exist; the role that ethical considerations of management, capital owners or staff play in the genesis of such strategies; whether there were specific scandals that triggered the decision to get engaged into CSR matters, etc. All these are very relevant questions for the analysis of those cases where living up to societal values and pursuing profits are not two mutually exclusive goals.

4.2 Further Research and Implications for Management and Investors

Consequently, future research could take these questions as the point of departure to leave the abstract level of analysis and narrow down the focus. To start with, all the explanations for a CSP/CFP-link provided in Sect. 3.3.1 could be scrutinised separately. Most interesting in this context is how various stakeholders *actually do change* their behaviour in response to positively or negatively perceived CSP of a certain company. People seldom argue against commonly accepted ethical standards when asked for their relevance. But it is a very different question whether these standards are equally relevant for their concrete *actions*, when these standards might stand in conflict with other relevant norms.

Industry-specific analyses could furthermore yield interesting results as to the conditions under which scandalous but widely spread business practices such as environmental pollution or human rights violation were finally abolished to the benefit of all stakeholders, including the shareholders. In this context, it is particularly important to gain insights into the actual decision processes and the underlying motivations of those taking the decisions. Case-studies and qualitative empirical research are methods that might be particularly helpful in delivering insights into such cases.

[1] Some would even argue that the average effects of a corporation's social performance are too small to have an impact on abstract financial performance measures, which would be noticeable in such studies. For an example of such an argument, cf. Vogel (2005), pp. 73.

The study offers some valuable results for both managers and investors who intend to include ethical considerations in their decisions. First, apart from the results directly derived from the analysis, it is equally interesting to consider what the study has *failed* to show. Only one of the CSP variables (*cust*) was negatively related to *Tobin's Q*; a result which in contrast to the others was not robust when measured against *roe*. Therefore, the analysis does *not* lend support to the Friedman-like arguments that consider CSR expenditures as an illegitimate waste of resources. This result is also relevant to investors who can assume that there is no penalty on SRI in the form of forgone profits. This is consistent with earlier findings concerning the performance of SRI funds.[2]

On the other hand, in the light of lacking support for the assumption of a causal link from social to financial performance, this study's results cannot be used to derive suggestions that investments in certain aspects of CSP are an economic imperative. As argued earlier, this study is not suitable for the justification of a purely instrumental view on CSR. Rather, it sheds some light on how managers should proceed concerning the development and implementation of CSR strategies. The analysis of the *de facto* performance within the sample revealed the interdependencies of past and actual CSP as well as that between single CSP components. This suggests that coherent CSR strategies should be pursued since there are strong interdependencies amongst the single dimensions and, at least in the case of environmental ratings, improvements cannot easily be accomplished. The results of the qualitative analysis are evenly important. They illustrate the necessity for management to thoroughly evaluate opportunities for a business case for CSR, given their very specific situation. This can include the examination of whether good CSP might be a source of competitive advantages or whether it is rather a means to avoid negative impacts of bad business conduct. Furthermore, it requires the analysis of which mediating effects are the strongest for the focal company. Who are the stakeholders mostly affected? Who can best benefit from which kinds of improvements? Are there enough market opportunities to be exploited or should one rather pursue action on an industry-wide level? How do these opportunities relate to the company's strengths? Even though this research cannot deliver full answers to such questions, it provides an applicable framework for their analysis and suggests some empirical evidence to be considered.

---

[2] Cf. Schröder (2004).

Appendix

Overview of variables used in the study

Variable name	Description	Cf. Section	Scaling	Source
Financial variables				
Tobin's Q	Market- to Book-Value in 2006; censored at the 95% quantile	3.1.2	Ratio	*Thomson Datastream/ Worldscope*
roe_{2005} *and* roe_{2006}	Retun on Equity in 2005 and 2006; censored at the 1 and 99% quantiles	3.1.3	Ratio	*Thomson Datastream/ Worldscope*
Control variables				
risk	CAPM's Beta for 2006, calculated by regressing company stock returns on market returns on a daily basis; values were mean-centered	3.1.3	Ratio	*Thomson datastream/ Worldscope*
lev	ratio of total debt to total assets; values were mean-centered	3.1.3	Ratio	*Thomson Datastream/ Worldscope*
size	Company size, measured by sales in 2006 (US$). Log values and mean-centered	3.1.3	Metrical	*Thomson datastream/ Worldscope*
CSR variables				
crr	Corporate responsibility rating	3.1.1	Binary	*oekom research AG*
scr	Social-cultural rating	3.1.1	Binary	*oekom research AG*
er	Environmental rating	3.1.1	Binary	*oekom research AG*
staff	Staff & suppliers	3.1.1	Binary	*oekom research AG*

(*continued*)

(continued)

Variable name	Description	Cf. Section	Scaling	Source
corpgov	Corporate governance & Business ethics	3.1.1	Binary	*oekom research AG*
enman	Environmental management & eco-efficiency	3.1.1	Binary	*oekom research AG*
cust	Customer & product responsibility	3.1.1	Binary	*oekom research AG*
soc	Society & community	3.1.1	Binary	*oekom research AG*
Interaction terms & other variables				
class	low (0) and high (1) impact industries		Binary	*oekom research AG*
cont	0 if Europe; 1 if North America or Australia	3.2.1	Binary	*oekom research AG*
cont2	1 if any other country	3.2.1	Binary	*oekom research AG*
enman × *class*	multiplicative term of *enman* and *class*	3.3.1	Binary	
enman × *size*	multiplicative term of *enman* and *size*	3.3.1	Metrical	
staff × *size*	multiplicative term of *staff* and *size*	3.3.1	Metrical	
corpgov × *size*	multiplicative term of *corpgov* and *size*	3.3.1	Metrical	

Note (concerning variables not referred to in this table): All *oekom* variables stem from ratings conducted in 2005/2006; "lagged" values refer to earlier ratings from 2002/2003. The subscript "Δ" denotes differences between these two ratings. Subscript "good" refers to performers better than the industry mean but lower than 0.75 quantile. "excellent" is for companies beyond 0.75 quantile.

References

Abbott WF, Monsen RJ (1979) On the measurement of corporate social responsibility: self-reported disclosure as a method of measuring corporate social involvement. Acad Manage J 22(3):501–515

Ackerman RW, Bauer RA (1976) Corporate social responsiveness. Harvard University Press, Cambridge, MA

Alberini A, Segerson K (2002) Assessing voluntary programs to improve environmental quality. Environ Resour Econ 22(1/2):157–184

Albers S, Hildebrandt L (2006) Methodische Probleme bei der Erfolgsfaktorenforschung – Messfehler, formative versus reflektive Indikatoren und die Wahl des Strukturgleichungs-Modells. Zeitschrift für betriebswirtschaftliche Forschung (zfbf) 58:2–33

Albinger HS, Freeman SJ (2000) Corporate social performance and attractiveness as an employer to different job seeking populations. J Bus Ethics 28(3):243–253

Alexander GJ, Buchholz RA (1978) Corporate social responsibility and stock market performance. Acad Manage J 21(3):479–486

Allouche J, Laroche P (2005) Responsabilité sociale et performance financière des entreprises: une synthèse de la littérature, Working paper. Universityé Paris 1 – Panthéon-Sorbonne

Anderson EW, Fornell CL, Donald R (1994) Customer satisfaction, market share and profitability. J Market 58(3):53–66

Anderson EW, Fornell C, Mazvancheryl SK (2004) Customer satisfaction and shareholder value. J Market 68(4):172–185

Anderson JC, Frankle AW (1980) Voluntary social reporting: an iso-beta portfolio analysis. Account Rev 55(3):467–479

Arellano M, Bond SR (1991) Some specification tests for panel data: Monte Carlo evidence and an application to employment equations. Rev Econ Stud 58(194):277–298

Arora S, Gangopadhyay S (1995) Toward a theoretical model of voluntary overcompliance. J Econ Behav Organ 28(3):289–309

Atkinson L, Galaskiewicz J (1988) Stock ownership and company contributions to charity. Admin Sci Q 33(1):82–100

Aupperle KE, Carroll AB, Hatfield JD (1985) An empirical examination of the relationship between corporate social responsibility and profitability. Acad Manage J 28(2):446–463

Backhaus K, Erichson B, Plinke W, et al (2006) Multivariate analysemethoden- eine anwendungsorientierte einführung, 11th edn. Springer, Berlin

Backhaus KB, Stone BA, Heiner K (2002) Exploring the relationship between corporate social performance and employer attractiveness. Bus Soc 41(3):292–318

Backman J (ed) (1975) Social responsibility and accountability. New York University Press, New York

Bagnoli M, Watts S (2003) Selling to socially responsible consumers: competition and the private provision of public goods. J Econ Manage Strat 12(3):419–445

de Bakker FGA, Groenewegen P, den Hond F (2005) A bibliometric analysis of 30 years of research and theory on corporate social responsibility and corporate social performance. Bus Soc 44(3):283–317

Ball E, Färe R, Grosskopf S, et al (2005) Manufacturing and corporate environmental responsibility: cost implications of voluntary waste minimisation. Struct Change Econ Dynam 16(3):347–373

Bansal P, Clelland I (2004) Talking trash: legitimacy, impression management, and unsystematic risk in the context of the natural environment. Acad Manage J 47(1):93–103

Barnett ML (2007) Stakeholder influence capacity and the variability of financial returns to corporate social responsibility. Acad Manage Rev 32(3):794–816

Barnett ML, Salomon RM (2006) Beyond dichotomy: the curvilinear relationship between social responsibility and financial performance. Strat Manage J 27(11):1101–1122

Barney J (1991) Firm resources and sustained competitive advantage. J Manage 17(1):771–792

Baron DP (2001) Private politics, corporate social responsibility, and integrated strategy. J Econ Manage Strat 10(1):7–45

Baron DP (2005) Corporate social responsibility and social entrepreneurship, Stanford Graduate School of Business, Research paper no. 1940, Standford, CA

Baron DP (2006a) Managerial contracting and corporate social responsibility Stanford Graduate School of Business, Research paper no. 1945, Stanford, CA

Baron DP (2006b) The positive theory of moral management, social pressure, and corporate social performance, Stanford Graduate School of Business, Research Paper No. 1940, Standford, CA

Bauer TN, Aiman-Smith L (1996) Green career choices: the influence of ecological stance of recruiting. J Bus Psychol 10(4):445–458

Bauer R, Guenster N, Otten R (2004) Empirical evidence on corporate governance in Europe: the effect on stock returns, firm value and performance. J Asset Manage 5(2):91–104

Becker-Olsen KL, Cudmore BA, Hill RP (2006) The impact of perceived corporate social responsibility on consumer behavior. J Bus Res 59(1):46–53

Benioff M (2004) Compassionate capitalism: how corporations can make doing good an integral part of doing well. Career Press, New Jersey

Berman SL, Wicks AC, Kotha S, et al (1999) Does stakeholder orientation matter? The relationship between stakehoder management models and firm financial performance. Acad Manage J 42(5):488–506
Blacconiere WG, Patten DM (1994) Environmental disclosures, regulatory costs, and changes in firm value. J Account Econ 18(3):357–377
Black B, Hasung J, Woochan K (2006) Does corporate governance predict firms' market values? Evidence from Korea. J Law Econ Organ 22(2):366–413
Bönning M (2004) Bewertung von Unternehmen – das Nachhaltigkeitsrating der oekom research AG. In: Dürndorfer M, Friederichs P (eds) Human capital leadership: Wettbewerbsvorteile für den Erfolg von morgen. Murmann, Hamburg, pp 413–426
Börsch-Supan A, Köke J (2002) An alied econometricians' view of empirical corporate governance studies. Ger Econ Rev 3(3):295–326
Bowen HR (1953) Social responsibilities of the businessman. Harper & Row, New York
Bowman EH (1973) Corporate social responsibility and the investor. J Contemp Bus 2(1):21–43
Bowman EH (1980) A risk/return paradox for strategic management. Sloan Manage Rev 21(3):17–31
Bowman EH, Haire M (1975) A strategic posture towards CSR. Calif Manage Rev 18(2):49–58
Bragdon JH, Marlin JA (1972) Is pollution profitable? Risk Manage 19(4):9–18
Brammer S, Pavlin S (2004) Building a good reputation. Eur Manage J 22(6):704–713
Branco MC, Rodriguez LL (2006) Corporate social responsibility and resource-based perspectives. J Bus Ethics 69(2):111–132
Brealey RA, Myers SC (2003) Principles of corporate finance, 7th edn. McGraw-Hill, Boston, p l
Breusch TS, Pagan AR (1979) A simple test for heteroskedasticity and random coefficient variation. Econometrica 47(5):1287–1294
Brown J, Fraser M (2006) Approaches and perspectives in social and environmental accounting: an overview of the conceptual landscape. Bus Strat Environ 15(2):103–117
Brown B, Perry S (1994) Removing the financial performance halo from fortune's 'most admired' companies. Acad Manage J 37(5):1347–1359
Brown TJ, Dacin PA (1997) The company and the product: corporate associations and consumer product responses. J Market 61(1):68–84
Browne MN, Haas PF (1974) Social responsibility: the uncertain hypothesis. MSU-Bus Top Summer 47–51
Cameron AC, Trivedi PK (2005) Microeconometrics and applications. Cambridge University Press, Cambridge
Carroll AB (1979) A three dimensional conceptual model of corporate performance. Acad Manage Rev 4(4):497–505

Carroll AB (1991a) Corporate social performance measurement: a commentary on methods for evaluating an elusive construct. In: Post JE (ed) Research in corporate social performance and policy, vol. 12. JAI, Greenwich, pp 385–402

Carroll AB (1991b) The pyramid of corporate social responsibility: toward the moral management of organizational stakeholders. Bus Horiz 34(4):39–48

Carroll AB (1999) Corporate social responsibility – evolution of a definitional construct. Bus Soc 38(3):268–295

Chamberlain N (1973) The limits of corporate responsibility. Basic Books, New York

Chatterji, AK, Levine D, Toffel MW (2007) How well do social ratings actually measure corporate social responsibility? Corporate Social Responsibility Initiative, Working paper no. 33, Cambridge, MA

Cheit EF (1964) The new place of business: why managers cultivate social responsibility. In: Cheit EF (ed) The business establishment. Wiley, New York

Chen KH, Metcalf RW (1980) The relationship between pollution control record and financial indicators revisited. Account Rev 55(1):168–177

Christmann P (2000) Effects of 'best practices' of environmental management on cost advantage: the role of complementary assets. Acad Manage J 43(4):663–680

Chung KH, Pruitt SW (1994) A simple approximation of Tobin's Q. Finance Manage 23(3):70–74

Claessens S, Djankov S, Fan JPH, et al (2002) Disentangling the incentive and entrenchment effects of large shareholdings. J Finance 57(6):2741–2771

Clarkson MB (1995) A stakeholder framework for analyzing and evaluating corporate social performance. Acad Manage Rev 20(1):92–117

Clarkson MB (1991) Defining, evaluating, and managing corporate social performance: the stakeholder management model. In: Post JE (ed) Research in corporate social performance and policy, vol. 12. JAI, Greenwich, pp 331–359

Cochran PL, Wood RA (1984) Corporate social responsibility and financial performance. Acad Manage J 27(1):42–56

Conner KR (1991) A historical comparison of resource-based theory and five schools of thought within industrial organization economics: do we have a new theory of the firm? J Manage 17(1):121–154

Core JE, Guay WR, Rusticus TO (2006) Does weak governance cause weak stock retruns? An examination of firm operating performance and investors' expectations. J Finance 61(2):655–687

Crane A, Matten D (2004) Business ethics – a European perspective. Managing corporate citizenship and sustainability in the age of globalization. Oxford University Press, Oxford

Crane A, McWilliams A, Matten D (eds) (2008) The Oxford handbook of corporate social responsibility. Oxford University Press, Oxford

Cryer EH, Ross WT (1997) The influence of firm behavior on purchase intention: do consumers really care about business ethics? J Consum Market 14(6):421–432

Davis K (1960) Can business afford to ignore social responsibilities? Calif Manage Rev 2(Spring):70–76

Davis K (1967) Understanding the social responsibility puzzle: what does the businessman owe to society? Bus Horiz 10(1):45–50
Davis K (1973) The case for and against business assumptions of social responsibilities. Acad Manage J 16(2):312–317
Davis K, Blomstrom RL (1966) Business and its environment. McGraw-Hill, New York
Davis K, Blomstrom RL (1971) Business, society, and environment: social power and social response. McGraw-Hill, New York
Deckop JR, Merriman KK (2006) The effects of CEO pay structure on corporate social performance. J Manage 32(3):329–342
Diamantopoulos A, Winklhofer HM (2001) Index construction with formative indicators – an alternative to scale development. J Market Res 38(2):269–277
Diltz JD (1995) The private cost of socially responsible investing. Appl Financ Econ 5(2):69–77
Donahue JA (1991) Ethics and institutions: a review essay. Relig Stud Rev 17(1):24–32
Donaldson T, Preston LL (1995) The stakeholder theory of the corporation: concepts, evidence, and implications. Acad Manage Rev 20(1):65–91
Dowell G, Hart S, Yeung B (2000) Do corporate global environmental standards create or destroy market value? Manage Sci 46(8):1059–1074
Drobetz W, Schillhofer A, Zimmermann H (2004) Corporate governance and expected stock returns: evidence from Germany. Eur Financ Manage 10(4):267–293
Drucker P (1984) The new meaning of corporate social responsibility. Calif Manage Rev 26:53–63
Du S, Bhattacharya CB, Sen S (2007) Reaping relational rewards from corporate social responsibility: the role of competitive positioning. Int J Res Market 24(3):224–241
Eberl M, Schwaiger M (2006) Segmentspezifischer Aufbau von Unternehmensreputation durch Übernahme gesellschaftlicher Verantwortung. Die Betriebswirtschaft (DBW) 66(4):418–440
Eells R, Walton CC (1974) Conceptual foundations of business. Irwin, Burr Ridge, IL
Elsas R (2003) Beta and returns revisited. Evidence from the German stock market. Int Financ Market Inst Money 13(1):1–18
Entine J (2003) The myth of social investing. A critique of its practice and consequences for corporate social performance research. Organ Environ 16(3):352–368
Epstein EM (1987) The corporate social policy process: beyond business ethics. Corporate social responsibility, and corporate social responsiveness. Calif Manage Rev 29:99–114
European Commission (2001) Promoting a European framework for corporate social responsibility, Green Paper COM (2001) 366, Brussels
European Commission (2002) Corporate social responsibility: a business contribution to sustainable development, communication from the Commission COM (2002) 347, Brussels

European Commission (2006) Implementing the partnership for growth and jobs: making Europe a pole of excellence on corporate social responsibility, Communication from the Commission COM (2006) 136, Brussels

Fitch HG (1976) Achieving corporate social responsibility. Acad Manage Rev 1(1):38–46

Flaherty M, Raaport A (1991) Multinational corporations and the environment: a survey of global practices, the center for environmental management. Tufts University, Medford

Fombrum CJ, Gardberg NA, Barnett ML (2000) Opportunity platforms and safety nets: corporate citizenship and reputational risk. Bus Soc Rev 105(1):85–106

Fombrum CJ, Shanley M (1990) What's in a name? Reputation building and corporate strategy. Acad Manage J 33(2):233–258

Frankfurt-Hohenheim, Projektgrue Ethisch-Ökologisches Rating/oekom research AG (eds) (2002) Ethisch-ölologisches Rating. Der Frankfurt-Hohenheimer Leitfaden und seine Umsetzung durch das Corporate Responsibility-Rating, Federführung: Johannes Hofman u. Claudia Döpfner, vol. 7, 2nd edn. Oekom Verlag, München

Frederick WC (1960) The growing concern over business responsibility. Calif Manage Rev 2:54–61

Frederick WC (1994) From CSR1 to CSR2: the maturing of business-and-society thought. Bus Soc 33(2):150–164

Frederick WC (1998) Moving to CSR4. Bus Soc 37(1):40–60

Freedman M, Jaggi B (1982) Pollution disclosures, pollution performance and economic performance. Omega 10:167–176

Freedman M, Jaggi B (1986) An analysis of corporate pollution disclosures included in annual financial statements on investors' decisions. In: Neimark M, Merino B, Tinker T (eds) Advances in public interest accounting, vol. 1. JAI, Greenwich, CT, pp 193–212

Freeman RE (1984) Strategic management – a stakeholder approach. Pitman, Boston

Freeman RE (1999) Divergent stakeholder theory. Acad Manage Rev 24(2):233–236

Freeman RE (2004) The stakeholder approach revisited. Zeitschrift für Wirtschafts- und Unternehmensethik (zfwu) 5(3):228–241

Friedman M (1962) Capitalism and freedom. University of Chicago Press, Chicago

Friedman M (1970) The social responsibility of business is to increase its profits. In: New York Times Magazine September 13, 32, reprinted in Hoffman WM, Frederick RE, Schwartz MS (eds) (2001) Business ethics. Readings and cases in corporate morality, 4th edn. New York, pp 156–160

Fry FL, Hock RJ (1976) Who claims corporate responsibility? The biggest and the worst. Bus Soc Rev 18(18):62–65

Fry LW, Keim GD, Meiners RE (1982) Corporate contributions: altruistic or for profit? Acad Manag J 25(1):94–106

Galaskiewicz J (1997) An urban grants economy revisited: corporate charitable contributions in the twin cities, 1979–81, 1987–89. Adm Sci Q 42(3):445–471

Glaser J, Hornung S, Labes M (2007) Indikatoren für die Humanressourcenförderung – Humankapital messen, fördern und wertschöpfend einsetzen. BAuA, Dortmund

Göbel E (2006) Unternehmensethik. Grundlagen und praktische Umsetzung. Lucius & Lucius, Stuttgart

Godfrey PC (2005) The relationship between corporate philanthropy and shareholder wealth: a risk management perspective. Acad Manage Rev 30(4):777–798

Gompers PA, Ishii JL, Metrick A (2003) Corporate governance and equity prices. Q J Econ 118(1):107–155

Goodpaster KE, Matthews JB Jr (1982) Can a corporation have a conscience. Harv Bus Rev 60(1):132–141

Gorton G, Schmid FA (2000) Universal banking and the performance of German firms. J Financ Econ 85(1):29–80

Graff Zivin J, Small A (2005) A modigliani-miller theory of altruistic corporate social responsibility. Top Econ Anal Policy 5(1):1–22

Grant RM (1991) The resource-based theory of competitive advantage. Calif Manage Rev 33(3):114–135

Graves SB, Waddock SA (1994) Institutional owners and corporate social performance. Acad Manage J 37(4):1034–1046

Graves SB, Waddock SA (2000) Beyond built to last ... stakeholder relations in 'built to last' companies. Bus Soc Rev 105(4):393–418

Greene WH (2003) Econometric analysis, 5th edn. Prentice Hall, New Jersey

Greening DW, Turban DB (2000) Corporate social performance as a competitive advantage in attracting a quality workforce. Bus Soc 39(3):254–280

Griffin JJ, Mahon JF (1997) The corporate social performance and corporate financial performance debate – twenty-five years of incomparable research. Bus Soc 36(1):5–31

Guerard JB Jr (1997) Is there a cost to being socially responsible in investing? J Invest 6(2):11–18

Gujarati DN (2003) Basic econometrics, 4th edn. McGraw-Hill, New York

Habisch A (2003) Corporate citizenship – Gesellschaftliches Engagement von Unternehmen in Deutschland. Springer, Berlin

Hair JF, Black WC, Babin BJ, et al (2006) Multivariate data analysis, 6th edn. Prentice Hall, New Jersey

Hamschmidt J, Dyllick T (2001) ISO 14001: profitable – yes! But is it eco-effective? Greener Manage Int 34(1):34–54

Hansen U, Schrader U (2005) Corporate Social Responsibility als aktuelles Thema der Betriebswirtschaftslehre. Die Betriebswirtschaft (DBW) 65(4):327–432

Harrisson JS, Freeman RE (1999) Stakeholders, social responsibility, and performance: empirical evidence and theoretical perspectives. Acad Manage J 42(5):479–485

Hart SL (1995) A natural resource-based view of he firm. Acad Manage Rev 20(4):986–1014

Hart SL, Ahuja G (1996) Does it pay to be green? An empirical examination of the relationship between emission reduction and firm performance. Bus Strat Environ 5(1):30–37

Heal G (2005) Corporate social responsibility. An economic and financial framework, The Geneva papers

Heinkel R, Kraus A, Zechner J (2001) The effect of green investment on corporate Behavior. J Financ Quant Anal 36(4):431–449

Henderson D (2001) Misguided virtue: false notions of corporate social responsibility. Institute of Economic Affairs, London

Henkel J (2000) The risk-return fallacy. Schmalenbach Bus Rev 52(4):363–373

Hermann A, Huber F, Kressmann F (2006) Varianz- und kovarianzbasierte Strukturgleichungsmodelle – Ein Leitfaden zu deren Spezifikation. Zeitschrift für betriebswirtschaftliche Forschung (zfbf) 58(1):34–66

Hillman AJ, Keim GD (2001) Shareholder value, stakeholder management and social issues: what's the bottom line. Strat Manage J 22(2):125–139

Hoenicke S (2002) Soziale Mindeststandards als Herausforderung an die Unternehmensführung. In: König M, Schmidt M (eds) Unternehmensethik konkret. Gesellschaftliche Verantwortung ernst gemeint. Gabler, Wiesbaden, pp 121–132

Höffe O (1993) Moral als Preis der Moderne. Suhrkamp, Frankfurt

Hoffmann J, Ott K, Scherhorn G (eds) (1997) Ethische Kriterien für die Bewertung von Unternehmen – Frankfurt-Hohenheimer Leitfaden. IKO, Frankfurt

Homann K, Pies I (1994) Wirtschaftsethik in der Moderne: zur ökonomischen Theorie der Moral. Ethik und Sozialwissenschaften 5(1):3–14

Hsiao C (2003) Analysis of panel data, 2 edn. Cambridge University Press, Cambridge

Hülsmann M, Müller-Christ G, Hasasis, H-D (eds) (2004) Betriebswirtschaftslehre und Nachhaltigkeit. Bestandsaufnahme und Forschungsprogrammatik. Deutscher Universitätsverlag, Wiesbaden

Hunter, JE, Schmidt FL (1990) Methods of meta-analysis: correcting errors and bias in research findings. Sage, Newbury Park, CA

Husted BW (2005) Risk management, real options, and corporate social responsibility. J Bus Ethics 60(2):175–183

Igalens J, Gond J-P (2005) Measuring corporate social performance in France: a critical and empirical analysis of ARESE data. J Bus Ethics 56:131–148

Ingram, RW, Frazier KB (1983) Narrative disclosures in annual reports. J Bus Res 11(1):49–60

Jaccard J, Turrisi R (2003) Interaction effects in multiple regression, 2nd edn. Sage, Thousand Oaks

Jann B (2005) Einführung in die Statistik, 2nd edn. Oldenbourg, München

Jarvis CB, MacKenzie SB, Podsakoff PM, et al (2003) A critical review of construct indicators and measurement model misspecification in marketing and consumer research. J Consum Res 30(2):199–218

Jensen MC (2002) Value maximization, stakeholder theory, and the corporate objective function. Bus Ethics Q 12(2):235–256

Johnson HL (1971) Business in contemporary society: framework and issues. Wadsworth, Belmont, CA

Johnson RA, Greening DW (1999) The effects of corporate governance and institutional ownership types on corporate social performance. Acad Manage J 42(5):564–576

Jones TM (1980) Corporate social responsibility revisited, redefined. Calif Manage Rev 12(2):59–67

Jones TM, Wicks AC, Freeman RE (2002) Stakeholder theory: the state of the art. In: Bowie NE (ed) The blackwell guide to business ethics. Blackwell, Malden, pp 19–37

Kakabadse A, Morsing M (eds) (2006) Corporate social responsibility. Reconciling aspiration with application. MacMillan, Hampshire

Kaplan SN, Zingales L (1997) Do investment-cash flow sensitivities provide useful measures of financing constraints? Q J Econ 112(1):169–216

Kirchhoff KR (2007) Das good company ranking. Corporate social responsibility Wettbewerb der 120 größten europäischen Konzerne. Kirchhoff Consult, Hamburg

Klassen RD, McLaughlin CP (1996) The impact of environmental management on firm performance. Manage Sci 42(8):1199–1214

Klassen RD, Whybark DC (1999) The impact of environmental management on firm performance. Acad Manage J 42(6):599–615

KLD Research (2007) Environmental, social and governance ratings criteria. SOCRATES – The corporate social ratings monitor, www.kld.com/research/data/KLD_Ratings_Methodology.pdf, accessed 07/07/15, Boston

Klein J, Dawar N (2004) Corporate social responsibility and consumers' attributions and brand evaluations in a product-harm crisis. Int J Res Market 21(3):203–217

Konar S, Cohen MA (2001) Does the market value environmental performance. Rev Econ Stat 83(2):281–289

Kotler P, Lee N (eds) (2005) Corporate social responsibility: doing the most good for your company and your cause. Wiley, Hoboken

KPMG Global Sustainability Services (2005) KPMG International survey of corporate responsibility reporting 2005, Amsterdam (KPMG Advisory)

Küer H-U (2006) Unternehmensethik. Hintergründe, Konzepte, Anwendungen. Schäffer-Poeschel, Stuttgart

Kurtz L, DiBartolomeo D (1996) Socially screened portfolios: an attribution analysis of relative performance. J Investing Fall 5(3):35–41

Kurucz EC, Colbert BA, Wheeler D (2008) The business case for corporate social responsibility. In: Crane A, McWilliams A, Matten D, et al (eds) The Oxford handbook of corporate social responsibility. Oxford University Press, Oxford, pp 83–112

La Porta R, Lopez-de-Silanes F, Shleifer A, et al (2002) Investor protection and corporate valuation. J Financ 57(3):1147–1170

Lang LHP, Litzenberger RH (1989) Dividend announcements: cash flow signalling vs. free cash flow hypothesis? J Financ Econ 24(1):181–191

Laszlo C (2003) The sustainable company: how to create lasting values through social and environmental performance. Island Press, Washington

Lenk H, Maring M (2004) Verantwortung. In: Schreyögg G, von Werder A (eds) (2004) Handwörterbuch Unternehmensführung und Organisation. Schäffer-Poeschel, Stuttgart, pp 1557–1565

Lerner LD, Fryxell GE (1988) An empirical study of the predictors of corporate social performance. J Bus Ethics 7(12):951–959

Lev B, Petrovits C, Radhakrishnan S (2006) is doing good for you? Yes, charitable contributions enhance revenue growth, New York University Stern School of Business Working Paper, New York

Levitt T (1958) The dangers of social responsibility. Harv Bus Rev 36(5):41–50

Levy FK, Shatto GM (1980) Social responsibility in large electric utility firms: the case for philanthropy. Research in corporate social performance and policy, vol 2. JAI, Greenwich, pp 237–249

Lindenberg EB, Ross SA (1981) Tobin's q ratio and industrial organization. J Bus 54(1):1–32

Lintner J (1965) The valuation of risk assets and the selection of risky investments in stock portfolios and capital budgets. Rev Econ Stat 47(1):13–37

Lohrie A, Merck J (2000) Sozialverantwortung im Handel – Praktische Erfahrungen beim Otto Versand unter besonderer Berücksichtigung des SA 8000. In: Bausch T, Kleinfeld A, Steinmann H (eds) Unternehmensethik in der Wirtschaftspraxis. Ham, München, pp 43–54

Luo X, Bhattacharya CB (2006) Corporate social responsibility, customer satisfaction, and market value. J Market 70(1):1–18

Maddox KE, Siegfried JJ (1980) The effect of economic structure on corporate philanthropy. In: Siegfried JJ (ed) The economics of firm size, market structure, and social performance. Bureau of Economics. Federal Trade Commission, Washington, DC, pp 202–225

Maignan I (2001) Consumers' perceptions of corporate social responsibilities: a cross-cultural comparison. J Bus Ethics 30(1):57–72

Maignan I, Ferrell OC, Hult TM (1999) corporate citizenship: cultural antecedents and business benefits. J Acad Market Sci 27(4):455–469

Manne HG, Wallich HC (1972) The modern corporation and social responsibility. American Enterprise Institute for Public Policy Research, Washington, DC

Margolis JD, Walsh JP (2003) Misery loves companies: rethinking social initiatives by business. Adm Sci Q 48(2):268–305

Matten D, Crane A (2005) Corporate citizenship: toward an extended theoretical conceptualization. Acad Manage Rev 30(1):166–179

Mattingly JE, Berman SL (2006) Measurement of corporate social action. Discovering taxonomy in the kinder Lydenberg domini ratings data. Bus Soc 45(1):20–46

Maxwell JW, Lyon TP, Hackett SC (2000) Self-regulation and social welfare: the political economy of corporate environmentalism. J Law Econ 43(2):583–618

McConnell JJ, Servaes H (1990) Additional evidence on equity ownership and corporate value. J Financ Econ 27(5):595–612

McGuire JB (1963) Business and society. McGraw-Hill, New York
McGuire JB, Dow S, Argheyd K (2003) CEO incentives and corporate social performance. J Bus Ethics 45(3):341–359
McGuire JB, Sundgren A, Schneeweiss T (1988) Corporate social responsibility and firm financial performance. Acad Manage J 31(4):854–872
McWilliams A, Siegel D (1997) Event studies in management research: theoretical and empirical issues. Acad Manage J 40(3):626–657
McWilliams A, Siegel D (2000) Corporate social responsibility and financial performance: correlation or misspecification? Strat Manage J 21(5):603–609
McWilliams A, Siegel D (2001) Corporate social responsibility: a theory of the firm perspective. Acad Manage Rev 26(1):117–127
Meyer JW, Rowan B (1991) Institutionalized organizations: formal structure as myth and ceremony. In: Powell WW, DiMaggio PJ (eds) The new institutionalism in organizational analysis. University of Chicago Press, Chicago, pp 41–62
Mintzberg H (1983) The case for corporate social responsibility. J Bus Strat 4(2): 3–16
Mitchell RK, Agle BR, Wood DJ (1997) Toward a theory of stakeholder identification and salience: defining the principle of who and what really counts. Acad Manage Rev 22(4):853–886
Mithas S, Krishnan MS, Fornell C (2005) Why do customer relationship management applications affect customer satisfaction? J Market 69(4):201–209
Mohr LA, Webb DJ, Harris KE (2001) Do consumers expect companies to be socially responsible? The impact of corporate social responsibility on buying behavior. J Consum Aff 35(1):45–72
Montgomery DB, Ramus CA (2003) Corporate social responsibility reputation effects on MBA job choice, Stanford GSB research paper no. 1805, Stanford
Morck R, Shleifer A, Vishny R (1988) Management ownership and market valuation. An empirical analysis. J Financ Econ 20(3):293–315
Morgan RM, Hunt SD (1994) The commitment-trust theory of relationship marketing. J Market 58(3):20–38
Moskowitz M (1972) Choosing socially responsible stocks. Bus Soc Rev 1(1):71–75
Mossin J (1966) Equilibrium in a capital asset market. Econometrica 34(4):768–783
Murray KB, Vogel CM (1997) Using a hierarchy of effects approach to gauge the effectiveness of CSR to generate goodwill towards the firm: financial versus nonfinancial impacts. J Bus Res 38(2):141–159
Norman W, MacDonald C (2004) Getting to the bottom of "triple bottom line". Bus Ethics Q 14(2):243–262
Nowak E, Rott R, Mahr TG (2005) Wer den Kodex nicht einhält, den bestraft der Kapitalmarkt? Eine empirische Analyse der Selbstregulierung und Kapitalmarktrelevanz des Deutschen Corporate Governance Kodex. Zeitschrift für Gesellschaftsrecht (ZGR) 34(2):252–279
Ogden S, Watson R (1999) Corporate social performance and stakeholder management: balancing shareholder and customer interests in the U.K. privatized water industry. Acad Manage J 42(5):526–538

Orlitzky M, Benjamin JD (2001) Corporate social responsibility and firm risk: a meta-analytic review. Bus Soc 40(4):369–396

Orlitzky M, Schmidt FL, Rynes SL (2003) Corporate social and financial performance: a meta-analysis. Organ Stud 24(3):403–441

Orsato R (2006) Competitive environmental strategies: when does it pay to be green? Calif Manage Rev 48(2):127–143

Oshana MAL (1997) Ascriptions of responsibility. Am Philos Q 34(1):71–83

Paine LS (2003) Value shift: why companies must merge social and financial imperatives to achieve superior performance. McGraw-Hill, New York

Palazzo G, Scherer G (2006) Corporate legitimacy as deliberation: a communicative framework. J Bus Ethics 66(1):71–88

Pava ML, Krausz J (1996) The association between corporate social-responsibility and financial performance: the paradox of social cost. J Bus Ethics 15(3):321–357

Peloza J (2006) Using corporate social responsibility as insurance for financial performance. Calif Manage Rev 48(2):52–72

Peterson DK (2004) The relationship between perceptions of corporate citizenship and organizational commitment. Bus Soc 43(3):296–319

Phillips RA, Freeman RE, Wicks AC (2003) What stakeholder theory is not. Bus Ethics Q 13(4):479–502

Picot A (1977) Betriebswirtschaftliche Umweltbeziehungen und Umweltinformationen. Grundlagen einer erweiterten Erfolgsanalyse für Unternehmungen. Duncker & Humblot, Berlin

Pierer Hv (2002) Gesellschaftliche Verantwortung wahrnehmen – Gründe und Erfahrungen eines global players. In: König M, Schmidt M (eds) Unternehmensethik konkret. Gesellschaftliche Verantwortung ernst gemeint. Gabler, Wiesbaden, pp 53–66

Porter ME, Kramer MR (2002) The competitive advantage of corporate philanthropy. Harv Bus Rev 80(12):56–69

Porter ME, Kramer MR (2006) Strategy & society: the link between competitive advantage and corporate social responsibility. Harv Bus Rev 84(12):78–92

Porter ME, van der Linde C (1995) Toward a new conception of the environment-competitiveness relationship. J Econ Perspect 9(24):97–118

Prahalad CK, Hamel G (1990) The core competence of the corporation. Harv Bus Rev 68(3):79–91

Preston LL (1978) Analyzing corporate social performance: methods and results. J Contemp Bus 7:135–150

Preston LL, O'Bannon DP (1997) The corporate social-financial performance relationship – a typology and analysis. Bus Soc 36(4):419–429

Pruzan P (1998) From control to values-based management and accountability. J Bus Ethics 17(13):1379–1394

Riess B (eds) (2006) Partner Staat? CSR-Politik in Europa. Bertelsmann Stiftung, Gütersloh

Riordan CM, Gatewood RD, Barnes B (1997) Corporate image: employees reactions and implications for managing corporate social performance. J Bus Ethics 16(4):401–412

Roberts, RW (1992) Determinants of corporate social responsibility disclosure: an application of stakeholder theory. Account Organ Soc 17(6):595–612

Roberts PW, Dowling GR (2002) Corporate reputation and sustained superior financial performance. Strat Manage J 23:1077–1093

Rodriguez P, Siegel D, Hillman AJ, et al (2006) Three lenses on the multinational enterprise: politics, corruption, and corporate social responsibility. J Int Bus Stud 37(6):733–747

Roman RM, Hayibor S, Agle BR (1999) The relationship between social and financial performance – repainting a portrait. Bus Soc 38(1):109–125

Ropohl G (1994) Das Risiko im Prinzip Verantwortung. Ethik und Sozialwissenschaften 5(1):109–120

Rowley TJ (1997) Moving beyond dyadic ties: a network theory of stakeholder influences. Acad Manage Rev 22(4):887–910

Rowley TJ, Berman SL (2000) A brand new brand of corporate social performance. Bus Soc 39(4):397–418

Ruf BM, Muralidhar K, Brown JJ, et al (2001) An empirical investigation of the relationship between change in corporate social performance and financial performance: a stakeholder theory perspective. J Bus Ethics 32(2):143–156

Ruf BM, Muralidhar K, Paul K (1998) The development of the systematic, aggregate measure of corporate social performance. J Manage 24(1):119–133

Russo MV, Fouts PA (1997) A resource-based perspective on corporate environmental performance and profitability. Acad Manage J 40(3):534–559

Salmones Ma del Mar García de los, Grespo AH, Bosque IR del (2005) Influence of corporate social responsibility on loyalty and valuation of services. J Bus Ethics 61(4):369–385

Schäfer H, Beer J, Zenker J, et al (2006) Who is who in corporate social responsibility rating? A survey of internationally established rating systems that measure corporate responsibility. Bertelsmann-Stiftung, Gütersloh

Schäfer H, Stederoth R (2002) Portfolioselektion und Anlagepolitik mittels Ethik-Filtern – Stand der empirischen Ergebnisse in der Kapitalmarktforschung. Kredit und Kapital 35(1):101–148

Schaltegger S, Synnestvedt T (2002) The link between 'green' and economic success: environmental management as the crucial trigger between environmental and economic performance. J Environ Manage 65:339–346

Scherer G, Palazzo G, Baumann D (2006) Global rules and private actors: toward a new role of the transnational corporation in global governance. Bus Ethics Q 16(4):505–532

Schneider D (1990) Unternehmensethik und Gewinnprinzip in der Betriebswirtschaftslehre. Zeitschrift für betriebswirtschaftliche Forschung (zfbf) 42(10):869–891

Schneider U, Steiner P (eds) (2004) Betriebswirtschaftslehre und gesellschaftliche Verantwortung. Mit Corporate Social Responsibility zu mehr Engagement. Gabler, Wiesbaden

Schröder M (2004) The performance of socially responsible investments: investment funds and indices. Financ Mark Portf Manage 18(2):122–142

Schuler DA, Cording M (2006) A corporate social performance-corporate financial performance behavioral model for consumers. Acad Manage Rev 31(3):540–558
Schwaiger M (2004) Components and parameters of corporate reputation – an empirical study. Schmalenbach Bus Rev 56(1):46–71
Schwartz MS, Carroll AB (2003) Corporate social responsibility: a three-domain approach. Bus Ethics Q 13(4):503–530
Scott WR (1995) Institutions and organizations. Thousand Oaks, California
Sen S, Bhattacharya CB (2001) Does doing good always lead to doing better? Consumer reactions to corporate social responsibility. J Market Res 38(2):225–243
Sethi SP (1975) Dimensions of corporate social performance: an analytical framework. Calif Manage Rev 17(3):58–65
Shane PB, Spicer BH (1983) Market response to environmental information produced outside the firm. Account Rev 58(3):521–538
Sharfman M (1996) The construct validity of the kld social performance data ratings. J Bus Ethics 15(3):287–297
Sharpe WF (1964) Capital asset prices: a theory of market equilibrium under conditions of risk. J Financ 19(3):425–442
Shrivastava P (1995) Ecocentric management for a risk society. Acad Manage Rev 20(1):118–137
Smith A (1991) Inquiry into the nature and causes of the wealth of nations, originally published in 1776. Prometheus Books, New York
Smith NC (2003) Corporate social responsibility: whether or how? Calif Manage Rev 45(4):52–76
Smith SM, Alcorn DS (1991) Cause marketing: a new direction in the marketing of corporate social responsibility. J Consum Market 8(3):19–35
Spencer BA, Taylor SG (1987) A within and between analysis of the relationship between corporate social responsibility and financial performance. Akron Bus Econ Rev 18(1):7–18
Spicer BH (1978a) Investors, corporate social performance, and information disclosure: an empirical study. Account Rev 53(1):94–111
Spicer BH (1978b) Market risk, accounting data, and companies' pollution control records. J Bus Financ Account 5(1):67–83
Spremann K (2003) Portfolio management, 2nd edn. Munich/Vienna
Staiger D, Stock JH (1997) Instrumental variable regression with weak instruments. Econometrica 65(3):557–586
Stanwick PA, Stanwick SD (1998) The relationship between corporate social performance and organizational size, financial performance, and environmental performance: an empirical examination. J Bus Ethics 17(2):194–204
Steinmann H (1973) Zur Lehre von der "Gesellschaftlichen Verantwortung der Unternehmensführung" – Zugleich eine Kritik des Davoser Manifests. Wirtschaftswissenschaftliches Studium 467–473
Stock JH, Watson MW (2007) Introduction to econometrics, 2nd edn. Pearson, Boston
Stock JH, Yogo M (2005) Testing for weak instruments in linear iv regression. In: Andrews DWK, Stock JH (eds) Identification and inference in econometric

models: a festschrift in honor of Thomas J. Rothenberg. Cambridge University Press, Cambridge, pp 80–108
Strahilevitz M, Myers JG (1998) Donations to charity as purchase incentives: how well they work may depend on what you are trying to sell. J Consum Res 24(4):434–446
Strawson G (1994) The impossibility of moral responsibility. Philos Stud 75:4–24
Sundaram AK, Inkpen AC (2004) The corporate objective revisited. Organ Sci 15(4):350–363
Süß S, Kleiner M (2006) Diversity-Management in Deutschland: Mehr als eine Mode? Die Betriebswirtschaft (DBW) 66(5):521–541
SustainAbility (ed) (2006) Buried treasures. Uncovering the business case for corporate sustainability. L&S Printing, London
Swanson DL (1995) Addressing a theoretical problem by reorienting the corporate social performance model. Acad Manage Rev 20(1):43–64
Swanson DL (1999) Toward an integrative theory of business and society: a research strategy for corporate social performance. Acad Manage Rev 24(3):506–521
Teoh HY, Shiu GY (1990) Attitudes towards corporate social responsibility and perceived importance of social responsibility information characteristics in a decision context. J Bus Ethics 9(1):71–77
Thompson JK, Smith HL (1991) Social responsibility and small business: suggestions for research. J Small Bus Manage 29(1):30–44
Tonge A, Greer L, Lawton A (2003) The enron story: you can fool some of the people some of the time. Bus Ethics Eur Rev 12(1):4–22
Turban DB, Greening DW (1997) Corporate social performance and organizational attractiveness to prospective employees. Acad Manage J 40(3):658–672
Ullman AA (1985) Data in search of a theory: a critical examination of the relationship among social performance, social disclosure and economic performance of US firms. Acad Manage Rev 10(3):540–557
Ulrich P (1999) Was ist "gute" Unternehmensführung? Zur normativen Dimension der Shareholder-Stakeholder-Debatte. In: Kumar BN, Osterloh M, Schreyögg G (eds) Unternehmensethik und die Transformation des Wettbewerbs. Shareholder-Value – Globalisierung – Hyperwettbewerb. Schäffer-Poeschel, Stuttgart, pp 27–52
Utting P (2000) Business responsibility for sustainable development, UNRISD occasional paper no. 2
Utting P (2005) Corporate responsibility and the movement of business. Dev Pract 15(3/4):375–388
Vance SC (1975) Are socially responsible corporations good investment risks? Manage Rev 64(8):19–24
Velamuri SR, Freeman RE (2006) A new approach to CSR: company stakeholder responsibility. In: Kakabadse A, Morsing M (eds) Corporate social responsibility. reconciling aspiration with application. Palgrave MacMillan, Hampshire, pp 9–23
Vogel DJ (2005) The market for virtue. The potential and limits of corporate social responsibility. Brookings Institution Press, Washington, DC

Votaw D (1973) Genius becomes rare. In: Votaw D, Sethi SP (eds) The corporate dilemma: traditional values versus contemporary problems. Prentice Hall, Englewood Cliffs, NJ, pp 11–45

Waddock SA (2000) Performance characteristics of social and traditional investments. J Invest 9(2):27–38

Waddock SA (2003) Myths and realities of social investing. Org Environ 16(3):369–380

Waddock SA, Graves SB (1997) The corporate social performance – financial performance link. Strat Manag J 18(4):309–319

Wagner M, Phu NV, Azomahou T, et al (2002) The relationship between the environmental and economic performance of firms: an empirical analysis of the European paper industry. Corp Soc Responsib Environ Manage 9:133–146

Wagner M, Schaltegger S (2004) The effect of corporate environmental strategy choice and environmental performance on competitiveness and economic performance: an empirical study of eu manufacturing. Eur Manage J 22 (5):557–572

Wagner M, Wehrmeyer W (2002) The relationship of environmental and economic performance at the firm level: a review of empirical studies in Europe and methodological comments. Eur Environ 12:149–159

Walgenbach P, Beck N, (2003) Effizienz und Anpassung. Das Erklärungspotenzial der neoinstitutionalistischen Organisationstheorie am Beispiel ISO 9000. Die Betriebswirtschaft (DBW) 63(5):497–515

Walton CC (1967) Corporate social responsibilities. Wadsworth, Belmont, CA

Wartick SL, Cochran PL (1985) The evolution of the corporate social performance model. Acad Manage Rev 10(4):758–769

Wartick SL, Rude RE (1986) Issues management: corporate fad or corporate function? Calif Manage Rev 29(1):124–132

Watson G (1996) Two faces of responsibility. Philos Top 24(2):227–248

Werner MH (2002) Verantwortung. In: Düwell M, Hübenthal C, Werner MH (eds) Handbuch der Ethik. Metzler, Stuttgart, pp 521–527

Wernerfelt B (1984) A resource-based view of the firm. Strat Manage J 5:171–180

Werther WB Jr, Chandler D (2006) Strategic corporate social responsibility – stakeholders in a global environment. Sage, Thousand Oaks

White H (1980) A heteroscedasticity consistent covariance matrix estimator and a direct test of heteroscedasticity. Econometrica 48(4):817–818

Wieland J (1999) Die Ethik der Governance. Metropolis, Marburg

Windsor D (2001) The future of corporate social responsibility. Int J Organ Anal 9(3):225–256

Wokutch RE, McKinney EW (1991) Behavioral and perceptual measures of corporate social performance. In: Post JE (ed) Research in corporate social performance and policy, vol. 12. JAI, Greenwich, pp 309–330

Wokutch RE, Spencer BA (1987) Corporate saints and sinners: the effects of philanthropic and illegal activity on organizational performance. Calif Manage Rev 29(2):62–77

Wolfe R (1991) The use of content analysis to assess corporate social responsibility. In: Post JE (ed) Research in corporate social performance and policy, vol. 12. JAI, Greenwich, pp 281–309

Wood DJ (1991a) Corporate social performance revisited. Acad Manage Rev 16(4):691–718

Wood DJ (1991b) Social issues in management: theory and research in corporate social performance. J Manage 17(2):383–406

Wood DJ (1995) The fortune database as a CSP measure. Bus Soc 34(2):197–198

Wood DJ, Jones RE (1995) Stakeholder mismatching: a theoretical problem in empirical research on corporate social performance. Int J Organ Anal 3(3):229–267

Wooldridge JM (2002) Econometric analysis of cross section and panel data. MIT, Cambridge, MA

World Business Council for Sustainable Development (2000) Corporate social responsibility: making good business sense, Geneve (World Business Council for Sustainable Development)

Zenisek TJ (1979) Corporate social responsibility – a conceptualization based on organizational literature. Acad Manage Rev 4(3):359–368

Zimmerli WC (1992) Wandelt sich die Verantwortung mit dem technischen Wandel? In: Lenk H, Ropohl G (eds) Technik und Ethik. Reclam, Stuttgart, pp 92–111

Zimmerman MJ (2001) Responsibility. In Becker LC, Becker CB (eds) Encyclopedia of ethics, vol. 2. Routledge, New York, pp 1486–1492

Index

FSC
www.fsc.org
MIX
Papier | Fördert
gute Waldnutzung
FSC® C083411

Kolibri 360 GmbH
Ferdinand-Jühlke-Straße 7
99095 Erfurt, Deutschland
produktsicherheit@kolibri360.de